LIVING JESUS

Growing In The **LIFE**
We Were Made To **LIVE**

Christian Families Today

A Christian Counseling and Training Ministry

ACKNOWLEDGEMENTS

CFT is a member of the Network 220 (www.network220.org). Some diagrams and content in this publication have been adapted from Network 220 conference materials.

Scripture quotations are taken from the New American Standard Bible®,
Copyright © 1960, 1962, 1963, 1968, 1971, 1972, 1973,
1975, 1977, 1995 by The Lockman Foundation
Used by permission. (www.Lockman.org)

Authors: Mark Fields, Tom Price, Greg Cleland, Ben Brezina, Ross O'Hair
Editors: Greg Brezina, Beau Brezina, Connie Brezina, Jamie Pharis Pyles, Swanee Ballman

COPYRIGHT

Copyright© 2019 by Christian Families Today
All rights reserved. Printed in the United States of America. No part of this book may be reproduced in any form or by any electronic or mechanical means including information storage and retrieval systems without permission in writing from the publisher, except by a reviewer who may quote brief passages in a review. To obtain permission(s) to use material from this work, please submit a written request to Christian Families Today.

Christian Families Today
174 Ashley Park Blvd STE 1, Newnan, GA 30263
Phone: 770-502-8050
E-mail: cft@CFTministry.org
www.ChristianFamiliesToday.org

Living IN Jesus Equipper's Guide
ISBN: 978-0-9773660-5-7

CONTENTS

INTRODUCTION

"The things which you have heard from me in the presence of many witnesses, entrust these to faithful men who will be able to teach others also."

2 Timothy 2:2

Welcome to the exciting journey of life equipping!

Most likely someone cared about your spiritual maturity and walked with you in your journey of growth. Now, our heavenly Father is leading you into intentional relationships to equip others to walk in intimacy with Him by living out of Christ's life.

Just as a newborn baby needs physical nourishment in order to grow and thrive, every born-again, spiritual infant needs to feed on truth. The Bible contains the truth we need to grow, but it is extremely helpful to see the truth explained and lived out in the life of a mature believer.

Jesus is the truth of God displayed in a physical body. One of the reasons He came to earth was for people to hear the voice of truth, see truth with their eyes, and touch truth with their hands. When Jesus ascended to heaven, the Father sent the Holy Spirit to live in those who believed in Jesus. They continued the ministry of Jesus and became the mouth, hands, and feet which God used to make more disciples. As a result, the making and maturing of disciples has spread not only around the world but also down through the generations.

God's plan is to fill the earth with His glory through the multiplication of His family who bear His image and contain His Spirit. In church circles, we call this multiplication process discipleship, mentoring, or training. In this study we have, instead, chosen the term "Life Equipping" (Eph. 4:12). God alone imparts life. Our role is to equip others with truth and encourage them to enjoy God's presence and express His life to others. Eventually, the people we equip will begin equipping others who, in turn, will invest in many more lives.

Lasting transformation and growth happen in close relationships between people who trust each other and share a common love and thirst to know Father more. The book of Acts records many public and powerful displays of evangelism; but the steady and continuous multiplication of the saints occurred in quiet, intimate relationships among Christians. They gathered in their homes, where one or two people led the others in growing in the grace and knowledge of Jesus Christ.

As you begin your journey of life equipping, we pray you grow personally, continue to receive God's revelation, and enjoy watching Father work in the life of others. Always remember our goal is to know God more intimately and respond in faith and obedience as He leads us in love. While gaining spiritual knowledge can appeal to the flesh by giving us a feeling of importance, love is what strengthens the church (1 Cor. 8:1; 13:1-2).

The enemy will work to prevent you and the participants from growing in dependence on the Father and expressing His life. You will be challenged and stretched in many ways – time constraints, distractions, inability to answer all questions asked, busyness, misunderstandings, and insecurity about your abilities or effectiveness. Remember who you are! God delights in you. He has pursued you, chosen you, and empowered you to be a Life Equipper (Rom. 15:14). The Holy Spirit lives in you and wants to lead you in this journey. Relax and receive from Father His grace, revelation, courage, and insight in your time of need. Enjoy what God is doing because you were made for "such a time as this."

HOW TO USE THIS BOOK

This *Living IN Jesus* Equipper's Guide has been designed to assist you, the equipper, as you walk with others through the *Living IN Jesus* Participant's Guide. This guide will help you think strategically about every session and provides you with questions to facilitate impactful discussions. Each session is structured to follow the outline of the *Living IN Jesus* Participant's Guide.

THEME

The theme captures, in one or two sentences, the main truth of the session. It is not intended to be read to the participants.

SUMMARY

The summary, taken directly from each session in the Participant's Guide, expands the theme to include the main teaching points. The summary, placed at the beginning of each session in the Equippers Guide, presents a high-level overview for preparation before examining the details of each truth.

 ## TRANSFORM REVIEW

The Transform questions in the Participant's Guide are designed for the participants to complete individually with the Holy Spirit after reading and reflecting on the truth in that session. Beginning in Session 2, the first question in every Connect section is, "What has God revealed to you since we last met?" This question provides an opportunity to review the previous week's Transform questions. As you share together in the presence of the Holy Spirit, your friendships will deepen.

In the Equipper's Guide, Transform questions from the previous session are included along with some explanations, examples, and possible follow-up questions. Reviewing the Transform questions provides the Equipper with important feed-back concerning the participants' comprehension of the material.

Each session is a stepping-stone to the next. As such, the sessions must be completed in order. It is necessary to understand all the previous sessions in order to move forward. If you discern that the participants have not understood some of the previous concepts, stop and address misunderstandings immediately rather than press on to meet a time schedule.

(Note: If the Holy Spirit leads, discuss the Transform questions at the end of the session instead of waiting until the beginning of the next.)

 ## CONNECT

Beginning in Session 2, the first Connect question encourages the participants to share what God taught them since the previous session. The remaining Connect questions relate to the session's topic. As the participants answer these questions, you will connect with them and gain insight into their current understanding. Approach this time with Spirit-led curiosity, resisting the urge to teach or correct; instead, focus on discovery. As you listen, make mental notes on how to teach or guide the participants in the Renew section.

If the participants do not understand the connect question, ask follow-up questions. In this Equipper's Guide, we have included possible follow-up questions for some of the more difficult questions.

RENEW

The Renew section provides the opportunity to communicate truths to renew the participants' minds. The intent is to explore the Biblical truths conversationally, emphasizing personal experience and application. This section is divided into titled subsections. This Equipper's Guide walks you through each subsection by providing a Key Point which help you focus on the main concept as you move through the material.

TEACHING METHODS

How you cover the truths in the Renew section is up to you and the Holy Spirit. Possible methods include:

- One participant reads each subsection (or paragraph if the subsection is long) aloud. After each reading, engage the participants (ask questions, look up selected scriptures, and discuss).

- The participants silently read the subsection (or paragraph) before questions and/or discussion.

- Participants read the session before they come to the study. Use the teaching time to review and go deeper by asking questions and giving illustrations.

- Explain the subsections and illustrations in your own words, and engage the participants continually. Encourage the participants to read the sessions as a form of review.

- In a classroom setting, divide the participants into small groups where each group reads and summarizes the subsections.

USING QUESTIONS EFFECTIVELY

However you decide to teach the truths in the Renew section, remember to use questions as much as possible. Questions engage the participants and probe for their understanding or agreement. Many of the subsection titles in the Renew section are written as questions. When you encounter a question, allow the participant time to answer before you examine the content of the subsection.

This Equipper's Guide has additional questions along with some guidance, which may be used to teach the material. If the participants struggle to answer a personal question, share from your own experience. In the discussions, depend on the Holy Spirit to supply relevant questions.

USING SCRIPTURE AS A FOUNDATION

Scripture is the foundation of the *Living IN Jesus* study. Much of the text in the Renew section includes scripture references where the truths can be found. The study will be richer if you take the time to look up and discuss at least some of the references. In your preparation, look up every reference so you can decide which ones will be most helpful to review during your session together.

HOW TO USE THIS BOOK

TEACHING TIPS AND CAUTIONS

Having taught these truths for over two decades both in the United States and worldwide, our ministry staff has uncovered common misunderstandings and potential pitfalls you may face as you work through this material. For this reason, we occasionally provide teaching tips and cautions.

 ## TRANSFORM

At the end of your session time together, encourage the participants to take time before the next session to review the materials and meditate as they answer the Transform questions. James 1:25 reveals a blessing for the one who looks intently on truth and becomes an effectual doer. The Holy Spirit illuminates the truth. Over time, meditating on truth produces a renewed mind and transformed behaviors. If there is confusion about how to answer these Transform questions, consider walking the participants through the first question as an example.

 ## PRAYER

Since relationship and intimacy with God involves conversation, we encourage you to incorporate both individual and group prayer into your study. Prayers are included at the end of every session in the Participant's Guide to stimulate conversation with God about the session's truths. Some people use these prayers as a group recitation prayer at the end of their session. Others have their own, spontaneous prayer time together and do not use our prayers. Follow the leading of the Spirit as you pray.

PREPARATION

Leading effective sessions involves the following preparations:

- Praying for the participants.

- Listening to the Holy Spirit's guidance.

- Reading the session in the Participant's Guide.

- Studying the corresponding session in the Equipper's Guide for helpful questions and tips.

- Looking up all scripture references provided.

- Making additional notes regarding any personal illustrations, questions, metaphors/analogies, etc.

SESSION TIME

These sessions are designed for 90 minutes. If your time frame does not allow for 90 minutes, split the sessions into manageable sections for your allotted time.

GROUP FORMATS

This study can be effective in a variety of formats. Smaller groups allow for more open and honest discussion. Larger groups can influence more people but may limit interaction. Here are some formats to consider:

- One-on-one

- Small group of 3 – 4 people (including Life Equipper)

- Couples group

- Classroom setting

AN EFFECTIVE LIFE EQUIPPER:

ENJOYS INTIMATE FELLOWSHIP WITH THE HEAVENLY FATHER

The equipper's purpose through this study is to help the participants experience more intimacy with God through Jesus Christ. If we are not walking with God in a personal relationship with intimate fellowship, then equipping anyone else becomes very difficult. They will clearly see that our words and our actions are in conflict. Our behavior may not always be perfect, but effective Life Equippers enjoy intimate fellowship with God and, like the Apostle Paul, desire to know God more fully (Phil. 3:8-11).

DEPENDS ON THE HOLY SPIRIT

The Holy Spirit alone reveals truth. God's truth is foolishness to those who are perishing (1 Cor. 1:18). We speak the words of truth under the leading of the Holy Spirit and leave the response up to God. Life Equippers might become discouraged or doubt their worth as a communicator if the participants do not understand the truths or the participants' lives are not transformed. Take those thoughts captive and enjoy sharing Christ's life without trying to get your needs met from the responses of others. We can only plant seeds; God causes the growth (1 Cor. 3:6).

INVESTS TIME TO DEVELOP RELATIONSHIPS

Life Equippers intentionally select people through the Holy Spirit's direction and invest the time to build relationships. Spending time together eating, talking, working, praying, playing, and serving provides the framework for building healthy relationships and communicating transformational truth.

CREATES A SAFE PLACE

People must have a safe place to talk openly and honestly about themselves. A safe place is one where:

- people accept one another (Rom. 15:7).
- judgment is suspended (Rom. 14:12-14).
- confidentiality is maintained (2 Tim. 2:16-17).
- grace is given (Eph. 4:29).
- people refrain from fixing and rescuing each other and allow the Holy Spirit to do the work (Phil. 2:12-13).
- authenticity and transparency are displayed and encouraged (2 Cor. 2:4).

In order to create a safe place, the equipper must be a safe person who is secure in their relationship with God and is confident in their identity in Christ. Equippers can exhibit these qualities and encourage others by creating a safe environment to learn and grow openly and honestly. If a safe group does not exist, consider meeting one-on-one with any participants who hinder the group.

SEES OTHERS AS GOD SEES THEM

God regards each believer as His creation in Christ, complete and perfected (2 Cor. 5:17; Heb. 10:14). God defines Christians, not by how we behave, but by what He has done on our behalf. God knows each of His children are on a maturing path of thoughts, beliefs, and behavior.

Effective Life Equippers see the participants in the same way as God. We recognize them as new creations and beloved children of God. We do not define them by their fleshly behavior patterns (2 Cor. 5:16), but see them based on their new heart to live out of Christ's life (Ezek. 36:26-27). We recognize their potential to mature as they grow in grace (2 Pet. 3:18). Adopting God's viewpoint of the participants enables us to listen, ask questions, and encourage the participants authentically and gracefully.

LISTENS INTENTLY

Because God is love, He is a listener (Ps. 34:15; 1 Pet. 3:12). To listen to someone is to love them. Mark 10:46-52 relates a great example of how Jesus loved through listening. God created all humanity with inner needs for acceptance and worth. The act of looking directly at people and giving them our undivided attention tells them that they matter.

Listening not only values others, but also allows us to gain knowledge and a better understanding of their thoughts, feelings, and heart (what is important to them) (James 1:19). Jesus listened intently and patiently to fully understand a person's position or belief on many occasions, including conversations with skeptical lawyers, scribes, Sadducees, and Pharisees (Matt. 22:23-28). As He discerned their false beliefs, He knew what truth to share with them.

Effective listening does not only involve paying attention to the words the other person speaks, it also involves listening to the Holy Spirit at the same time. Since we can listen three to four times faster than a person speaks, we have plenty of capacity to tune into the Holy Spirit's insight and direction.

Listening to the Holy Spirit is not the same as focusing on how we are going to respond to what they have said so we can solve their problems for them (fix them). Listening to the Spirit as we listen to others enables us to discern true thoughts and beliefs shared in the conversation. Jesus did this masterfully with the Pharisees (Luke 5:21-22).

Effective listening also involves looking at energy (voice tone, speed, volume, etc.) in the other person's expression. Body language is another important way we communicate. People will sometimes communicate with their facial and body positioning what they are unwilling to say with their words.

ASKS GOOD QUESTIONS

Asking effective questions is an integral part of good listening and a powerful way to communicate truth in love. Partnered with good listening, asking questions values people by letting them know they matter and that we are interested in what they are saying. Plus, asking questions communicates to others we believe in their ability to think for themselves.

Asking questions generates interest and invites engagement. As a Life Equipper, asking questions allows you to assess prior knowledge and discover which specific truths need addressing in depth. Good questions direct the participants' focus on important truths and open an avenue for the Holy Spirit to illuminate.

God wants His truth to tear down the strongholds of lies which exists in every mind. Questions, more than answers, powerfully steer our thinking. Knowing and believing His truth makes us free. A well-timed question can expose lies in our current beliefs and stimulate us to walk in truth.

Jesus mastered the skill of asking questions. Sometimes He would even answer a question with a question in order to bring the person into deeper engagement (Luke 10:25-26, 36-37).

QUALITIES OF AN EQUIPPER

SUPPORTS AND ENCOURAGES

When truth is spoken in love, people are built up and encouraged instead of torn down and discouraged (1 Thess. 5:11,14). Truth spoken in love gives grace or favor to those who hear (Eph. 4:29). Avoid using shameful messages to address behaviors or answers. One powerful way to support and encourage other believers is to reinforce their identity in Christ (Session 10). Even if participants stumble, a Life Equipper is quick to acknowledge God's love and forgiveness and speak life to them, demonstrating unconditional love for them.

CORRECTS IN HUMILITY AND GENTLENESS

Confronting a brother or sister about sin is sometimes necessary when we see fleshly behaviors stemming from false beliefs. During these times, love directs us to challenge and reprove in humility and gentleness (Gal. 6:1a; Eph.4:2-3, 15a, 29). Truth spoken in love never heaps guilt or shame on another person. Christ took our guilt and shame on the cross (Rom. 8:1). The Life Equipper's message will be helpful when conveyed in love, as it considers the participants' best interest and outcome. Correction in love will always be positive and growth-oriented. Love "bears all things, believes all things, hopes all things, endures all things" (1 Cor. 13:7).

Jesus corrected many people who were sinning, and His correction was usually gentle. Even a bruised reed, He did not break (Matt. 12:20). His gentleness and grace shone brightly with the woman caught in adultery. When everyone else sought to stone her, He forgave her even as He instructed her to stop sinning (John 8:11).

COMMUNICATES TRUTHS IN RELEVANT WAYS

Speaking the truth in love means we search for ways to communicate truth to make it relevant and impactful to another person. Effective Life Equippers seek to discover the participants' current understanding, join them, and relate to them at their level (Col. 4:4, 6). Strive to communicate truth as it applies to life instead of just theoretical knowledge. Jesus was a master communicator. He effectively used parables (Mat. 13:3), object lessons (leaven – Mark 8:15; mustard seed – Mat. 13:31-32, fig tree - Mat. 21:18-22), and teachable moments (widow's mite – Mark 12:41-44) to equip His disciples.

SERVES WITH HUMILITY

Serving another person communicates love in a powerful way. Sometimes acts of kindness preach the truth more loudly than words. While the disciples were arguing over who was the greatest, Jesus preached a powerful truth to them by washing their feet (Luke 22:24; John 13:3-9). His act of service delivered the powerful and transformative truth that the greatest in God's kingdom will be the servant of all (Matt. 20:26). An effective Life Equipper serves in kindness (Gal. 5:13; Phil. 2:1-4) by bearing other's burdens (Gal. 6:2), praying for others often (Eph. 6:18-19), and sharing in other's joys and sorrows (Rom. 12:15; 1 Cor. 12:6).

The Apostle Paul encouraged the Philippians to "do nothing from selfishness or empty conceit, but with humility of mind regard one another as more important than yourselves" (Phil. 2:3). Effective equippers are humble and resist the temptation to find their identity in ministry. True humility is not thinking about yourself and your needs when you are relating to others. When we look to our Heavenly Father to meet all our needs for worth and value, we are set free from trying to establish our worth from a position of leadership or our role as an equipper.

Depending on God and walking in humility also opens more doors for effective ministry. People resist those who pridefully set themselves over others and come across as arrogant experts. On the other hand, there is an attractiveness to the humble believer who depends on God and shares the fruit of love, joy, peace, patience, kindness, goodness, faithfulness, gentleness and self-control.

1. How do I respond to someone who does not have the correct answer to a question I ask?

Everyone differs in personality, but we all want to feel worthwhile and valuable. No one likes to be mocked or feel like they are stupid. Try to find ways to encourage the participants and lead them to the truth. Validate their attempt at answering before saying it is not exactly the answer you were searching for (e.g., "I like when you said [repeat what they said]. And what do you think about [state the truth]?" "I appreciate your thoughts. Another way to look at it might be …"). If possible, use follow-up questions to re-direct the participants to the truth. It may be possible they have not understood your question. A good way to deflect some of the embarrassment of receiving a wrong answer is to take responsibility for the possibility that you may not have communicated the question effectively (e.g., "I may not have communicated clearly. Let me ask the question this way."). The Holy Spirit will give you wisdom in the moment as to how to speak the truth in love.

2. How do I deal with participants who disagree with my theology?

- Understand your motives - "Am I reacting to their disagreement out of fleshly desire, or am I walking in the Spirit?" "Am I looking for respect from the participants?" "Am I holding onto the need to be right?"

- Decide if the issue is important enough to address at this time - "Is this disagreement about a foundational truth on which the *Living IN Jesus* study is based?" If not, postpone the discussion until a more appropriate time.

- Understand your perspective - "Why do I believe what I believe?" "What scripture supports my perspective?" "God, what is Your perspective and direction?"

- Understand their position - Ask follow-up questions to fully understand their position. "What has led you to this belief?" "On what do you base your opinion?"

- Ask permission to engage the disagreement - Permission builds relational capital. The relationship is more important than being right.

3. How can I deal with participants who consistently change the subject?

Re-direct the discussion back to the original topic. If the participants continue to change the subject, stress the value of your time together and emphasize the subject's value for personal transformation.

4. What if the participants do not answer the Transform questions?

- On the first or second occurrence, answer the Transform questions together at the beginning of the session.

- If the participants do not answer the Transform questions on a regular basis, without condemnation, ask what keeps them from answering the questions. Address the participants' answers, considering their legitimate hindrances and their motivations (true desire to continue the study). Do not assume the participants' different learning styles indicate their true motivation.

- Completing the Transform questions in writing may not be the best method for all participants. State the purpose of the Transform section. Ask the participants, "What method works for you?" Honor the participants by reviewing the questions according to their preferred method.

5. What if the participants regularly cancel or postpone sessions?

Ask the participants for the reason they must cancel or postpone. There may be illness, family concerns, changes in schedule, etc. Discuss options to meet at other times or postpone the study until the participants are able to continue. If the participants seem to avoid certain sessions, explain that some of the sessions are more difficult. Reinforce the importance of those sessions. Ask questions to find their reasons for missing those sessions. Avoid shaming or condemning questions or tone. If the participants seem to lose energy (enthusiasm or desire), address their change in desires and ask what they are willing to do regarding studying *Living IN Jesus*.

6. What if the participants forget some of the basic concepts covered in previous sessions (e.g., 10 sessions into the study and they still mistake the difference between a need and a desire or forget that God is the One who meets all needs)?

When you recognize the participants' lack of understanding, go back to the session in question and review any topic not clearly understood. Ask the participants questions that show you the specific areas where they do not understand the truth. Review the verses, use illustrations, or personal disclosure as the Holy Spirit leads.

7. What if the participants claim they have forgiven others, surrendered rights, or understood their flesh patterns, but it becomes apparent they have not?

Refer to the participants' statement which leads you to think they have not understood, believed, and applied the truth. Ask the participants to tell you more about that statement. Use questions to connect the truth to the fact that they have not forgiven others, surrendered rights, or understood their flesh patterns.

CONCEPT OF GOD
Life

THEME

God is Life.

SUMMARY

God is life, spirit, and love. He is also the creator and the personal relater. All He creates flows from His essence. Knowing and possessing God's character and nature are essential to experiencing a personal relationship and intimate fellowship with Him.

CONNECT   (10 min.)

ASK **How would you describe God?**

Listen for the participants' concept of God. If you do not get a response, probe further by offering descriptive words or adjectives about God. (e.g., "Would you say God is distant...fair...judgmental...loving...etc.?")

ASK **How did you come to believe that?**

Listen for the influences other than the Bible that helped form and shape the participants' concept of God. This information may help you understand the participants' flesh when you get to Sessions 7 and 15.

ASK **How would you go about finding out what God is really like?**

This question will help you understand the participants' knowledge, trust, and comfort with the Bible as a source of understanding God. *Living IN Jesus* is built upon Scripture. Reading the Scripture references will help solidify the participants' comfort with and trust in the Bible.

> **TEACHING TIP:**
> Remember to listen, not teach. The priority during the "Connect" time is building relationship, not correcting the participants.

RENEW   (60 min.)

GOD IS ETERNAL LIFE

ASK **What is eternal life?**

Some may say that eternal life is a life that is attained after we physically die. Other answers may include heaven, a destination or place, life that does not end,

> **KEY POINT:**
> God is the definition of eternal life. When God gives life, He is giving Himself.

a quality of life, etc. The word eternal is defined as "without end or beginning." God is eternal life.

> **ASK** How does the fact that God is eternal impact your view of Him?

> **ASK** How does the fact that God is eternal affect your relationship with Him?

GOD IS SPIRIT

> **ASK** How has God made Himself known to you?

Help the participants explore how a God, who is spirit, is able to connect with His physical creation. Possible answers: Scripture, the beauty of nature, thoughts, dreams, circumstances, other people, etc.

> **ASK** How does the fact that God is spirit affect your relationship with Him?

GOD IS LOVE

> **ASK** What is love to you?

> **ASK** How does God's love differ from other types of love?

Emphasize that God's love is the only love that is unconditional.

> **ASK** What is the most meaningful characteristic of God's love to you?

After going through the aspects of God's love, this question is an opportunity to see how the Holy Spirit is speaking to the participants.

> **ASK** How does the fact that God is love impact your relationship with Him?

GOD IS CREATOR

> **ASK** What in creation gives evidence of God's wisdom, imagination, and power?

Possible answers: mountains, sunsets, complex creatures, the human eye, etc.

> **ASK** How does the fact that God is creator impact your relationship with Him?

GOD IS RELATER

> **ASK** What characteristics of the relationship between the Father, Son, and Holy Spirit do you see?

> **ASK** How does the fact that God is a relater affect your relationship with Him?

TEACHING TIP: God transcends the physical universe He created. He is infinite and uncontained.

TEACHING TIP: The very essence of God is LOVE which is manifested through the life of Jesus.

TEACHING TIP: Everything that exists has come from God's wisdom, imagination, and power.

TEACHING TIP: God is a relational being comprised of three distinct Persons, who enjoys a harmonious loving relationship within Himself.

ILLUSTRATION: GOD IS A TRINITY

In this study, a triangle is used to represent God. A triangle is one shape consisting of three distinct points. The Father is placed at the top to signify his functional role as leader (Gal. 4:4), protector (Ps. 68:5) and provider (Matt. 7:11). Rays of light are behind the word "Father" because He is the "Father of lights" (James 1:7) and He "dwells in unapproachable light" (1 Tim. 6:16).

TRANSFORM

After meeting together, the Transform questions allow the participants to process the session's truths on their own. Review the participants' answers with them at the beginning of the next session.

(**Note**: If the Holy Spirit leads, discuss the Transform questions at the end of the session instead of waiting till the beginning of the next.)

PRAYER   (10 min.)

Since relationship and intimacy with God involves conversation, we encourage you to incorporate both individual and group prayer into your study.

DESIGN OF HUMANITY
Containers of Life

THEME

Humanity was designed to contain God's life.

SUMMARY

Adam and Eve were made in the image of God, thus their core identity was "child of God." God uniquely designed humans as living beings who are each a spirit and soul (in His image), dwelling in a physical body and expressing themselves through their soul (with thoughts, emotions, and choices) and body (according to His likeness). As a result of this design, Adam and Eve enjoyed a personal relationship and intimate fellowship with God.

TRANSFORM REVIEW (10 min.)

1. How did authority figures and/or religious teaching shape my concept of God in my formative years?

After hearing the answer, explore any misconceptions the participants may believe regarding their concept of God. Any wrong concept will affect how they receive truth presented in the rest of this study. Address influences that helped shape their beliefs. Many of us develop a concept of God by projecting onto Him a flawed image derived from authority figures (e.g., An absentee father can foster the concept of an absent or aloof God. A harsh mother can develop an idea of God as harsh or judgmental.).

2. Has my concept of God changed? If so, what influences have shaped my present concept of God?

The purpose of this question is to understand where the participants are on their journey with God (e.g., How much do the participants know about God? How much do the participants want to know?). Are there certain influences stimulating the participants to seek the Lord in a more intimate way? A good follow-up question might be, "What should influence our concept of God?"

3. What attribute of God comforts me the most? Why?

This question provides an opportunity for the participants to reflect on God and His attributes. Join the participants with a sense of awe and wonder to help stimulate a desire for greater intimacy with God.

> **TEACHING TIP:**
> Before beginning today's lesson, review the transform questions from Session 1: Concept of God. The participant should have answered these alone before coming together for this session.

4. Which of His attributes do I have trouble embracing? Why?

Answering this question helps to address questions and perhaps doubts regarding God, His character and nature.

5. What does a personal relationship and intimate fellowship with God look like to me?

This question allows participants to internalize and express what they learned in the session and to enjoy a personal relationship and intimate fellowship with God.

CONNECT   (10 min.)

 TEACHING TIP:
Remember to listen, not teach.

ASK   **What has God revealed to you since we last met?**

This question opens discussion of any additional revelations not covered in the Transform review.

ASK   **What is a human being?**

Listen for where the participants place emphasis. Are they focused on the physical, spiritual, or psychological aspect of humans?

ASK   **What are the components of a human being?**

Make a mental note of missing component(s) (body, soul, and/or spirit), so you can emphasize it in the Renew section.

ASK   **Who are you? Describe yourself in three sentences.**

Where do the participants currently place their identity? Listen for identities based on role, gender, performance, occupation, relationships, etc.

RENEW   (60 min.)

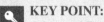 **KEY POINT:**
Adam and Eve were each created with an identity in their inner being which was a direct reflection of God. Thus, they were identified as children of God, and behaved like Him.

HUMANITY'S IDENTITY ESTABLISHED

ASK   **What is identity?**

Before going through the content, ask this question, which allows the participants to think about identity – "who or what a person is."

ASK   **Why is knowing your identity important?**

This question emphasizes why this session begins with the explanation of identity. Knowing and believing who you are (image/identity) impacts what you do (likeness/behavior).

THE INNER BEING OF HUMANS INCLUDES A SPIRIT...

ASK **How have you experienced God in your spirit?**

Some may say they never have. It may help to share your experiences of enjoying God in your spirit. Possible answers: thoughts about God's truth that release joy within you; an undeniable pressure or impression of His presence, voice, or direction; an impression so strong it leads to action; etc. This is covered in more detail in Session 11.

 Caution: Many people do not see themselves as a being who has a spirit. They will more likely view themselves as a physical being who can act spiritual (behavior). These two views are not the same. A physical being can act spiritual because he or she has an inner being which includes a spirit.

...WITH SPIRITUAL SENSES...

ASK **How did Adam and Eve interact with God?**

Lead the participants to acknowledge the uniqueness of humanity's design, enabling them to communicate intimately with God. We do not know the exact way God communicated with Adam and Eve, but it is clear when God gave commands to or asked questions of Adam and Eve (Gen. 3), they clearly received and understood His communication.

...DESIGNED TO WORK IN AND WITH GOD'S SPIRIT

ASK **What are the benefits of having God's Spirit living in you?**

Possible answers: a personal relationship and intimate fellowship with God; accessibility to power, wisdom, life, guidance, comfort, and all of the fruit mentioned in Galatians 5:22-23; etc.

THE INNER BEING OF HUMANS INCLUDES A SOUL

ASK **How have you experienced another person's soul through your interactions in relationships?**

Possible answers: Their thoughts become words. Their emotions can be heard in their voice tone or seen in their body language. Their decisions can be seen by their next course of action. Etc.

HUMANS LIVE IN BODIES

ASK **What do you like about having a physical body?**

Possible answers: We can enjoy God's beautiful creation (through the senses). We have the ability to create, to labor, and to oversee God's creation. We can enjoy human relationships, Etc.

KEY POINT: It was necessary for God to create a spirit in human beings in order to have an intimate relationship with God, who is Spirit.

KEY POINT: God created humanity with spiritual senses in order to interact with Him.

KEY POINT: God designed humanity to express His nature by placing His Spirit inside them.

KEY POINT: God designed humans with a soul to think, feel, and make decisions.

KEY POINT: Our physical bodies are the containers through which we can interact with our environment on this earth.

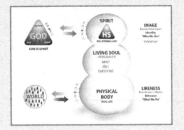

ILLUSTRATION: HUMANITY'S UNIQUE DESIGN

Review the guide to this illustration on page 153 of the *Living IN Jesus* Participant's Guide. The concept of God [illustrated by the triangle icon] was covered in Session 1. Start with "image" and "likeness" on the right side.

TRANSFORM

After meeting together, the Transform questions allow the participants to process the session's truths on their own. Review the participants' answers with them at the beginning of the next session.

PRAYER   (10 min.)

Since relationship and intimacy with God involves conversation, we encourage you to incorporate both individual and group prayer into your study.

NEEDS OF HUMANITY
Supplied Life

3

THEME

God supplies His life to meet inner needs.

SUMMARY

God designed humanity with needs only He can meet. This design established an intimate relationship characterized and enhanced by man's dependence on God's provision. Adam and Eve lived in a healthy relationship with God (loving Him), with themselves (loving themselves), and each other (based on unconditional love and enjoyment of His overflow to each other).

TRANSFORM REVIEW (10 min.)

1. What does it mean to me that I contain God's life?

Use a follow-up question to apply their answer to their everyday circumstances, attitudes, desires, and/or choices (e.g., If they respond, "Containing God's life means God is always with me.", you might ask, "How does knowing God is always with you affect the way you interact with others?").

2. What importance, or value, do I place on my spirit?

Session 2 is designed for the participants to learn to see themselves as more than physical beings. Their responses here are a gauge to see how much they understand the concepts in that session.

3. What might keep me from acknowledging this part of me?

Since the material world is so influential, this question explores those beliefs and/or circumstances that keep the participants from embracing this truth.

4. If I have spiritual ears, in what ways do I hear God speak to me?

The unbeliever cannot accept the things of the spirit of God (1 Cor. 2:14). If a person is a believer, then he/she has spiritual ears. This question gives the participants a chance to acknowledge those times they have heard God. If a person says he or she has not heard from God, this would be a good opportunity to share how you recognize God's voice.

> **TEACHING TIP:**
> Before beginning today's lesson, review the transform questions from Session 2: Design of Humanity. The participant should have answered these alone before coming together for this session.

5. When God speaks to me, what emotions do I feel? What thoughts enter my mind? What decisions do I make in response?

This question is designed to get the participants to make the connection with emotions, thoughts, and decisions in relation to God. If necessary, help them make this association. Use specific examples or events to help make the connection. If the participants' answers are too general, ask for details about a particular time when they heard from the Lord.

6. Take some time to listen. What is the Holy Spirit telling me in this session?

This question is used frequently in the Transform sections of the *Living IN Jesus* study. Continually encourage the participants to listen to the Holy Spirit for further, specific illumination. The Holy Spirit will never tell us something that contradicts Scripture.

 CONNECT (10 min.)

• • • • • • • • • • • • • • • • • • •

 TEACHING TIP:
Remember to listen, not teach.

ASK What has God revealed to you since we last met?

This question opens discussion of any additional revelations not covered in the Transform review.

ASK What does the phrase "Supplied Life" mean to you? Who or what is the supplier?

Listen for the participants' concept of both "supply" and "life". If the participants do not understand that God is life, refer back to Session 1, Concept of God (God is Eternal Life).

ASK What makes you feel alive? What is satisfied inside you that generates those feelings?

Listen for how they connect feeling alive with having a need met.

 RENEW (60 min.)

• • • • • • • • • • • • • • • • • • •

KEY POINT:
God created Adam needy and dependent.

GOD CREATED ADAM (MAN) WITH NEEDS

ASK How do you react to the fact that you are needy?

If the participants respond negatively, refer to their physical needs. We all need air, food, and water for physical life. Neediness does not imply a person is inferior or defective.

WHAT IS A NEED?

ASK Let the participants answer the title question before reading the paragraph.

 Caution: The participants may confuse the concepts of need and desire. The distinction between these two is discussed later in this session. If possible, wait to discuss that concept until you come to the sub-section "What Is The Difference Between Need And Desire?" If the distinction must be made now, go to that sub-section for clarification.

> **KEY POINT:**
> A need is something that must be met in order to live.

WHAT ARE THOSE INNER NEEDS?

ASK Let the participants answer the title question before reading the paragraph.

This question challenges the participants to be aware of their needs by naming these needs.

ASK What other needs might a man have that are not listed in the sub-section?

The participants' answers may not be a need, but a desire. The difference is covered in "What Is The Difference Between Need And Desire?" You can address this topic now or wait until that sub-section. This question focuses on a man's inner needs. The inner needs of women will be discussed later in this session.

ASK How is your list of inner needs connected to the need for worth or value?

The participants list is directly connected to their need to feel worthwhile. When we believe we are loved and respected, we feel worthwhile or valued.

> **KEY POINT:**
> Though we have many inner needs, they can be summarized in the need for worth.

WHO IS SUPPOSED TO MEET HUMANITY'S NEEDS?

ASK Let the participants answer the title question before reading the paragraph.

ASK Tell me about a time when you experienced God meeting an inner need. How did God do that?

This question connects the truth stated in the sub-section with the participants' experience. If they answer that God used another person, acknowledge the value of God's use of others to communicate His provision. This question may be a good transition to the next sub-section "What Is The Difference Between Need And Desire?". God does use others to meet our needs, and we also enjoy the fulfilled desire of connecting with others. The danger lies in depending on others to meet our needs. If the participants struggle to answer, share how God has met your needs.

> **KEY POINT:**
> Only God is qualified to meet our needs effectively.

🔑 **KEY POINT:** A need is something that MUST be met to live as God designed, but a desire is the yearning for something. A need is always desired, but a desire is not always a need.

🔑 **KEY POINT:** God designed Adam with needs to establish a relationship characterized by God's provision and Adam's dependency.

🔑 **KEY POINT:** God fashioned Eve for a personal relationship with Him and intimate fellowship with Adam.

🔑 **KEY POINT:** Women may rank their inner needs differently than men, but their needs can also be summarized in the need for worth.

WHAT IS THE DIFFERENCE BETWEEN NEED AND DESIRE?

ASK Let the participants answer the title question before reading the paragraph.

ASK What are some examples of a desire that is not a need?

Possible examples: a desire for a compliment from a friend, a desire for sexual intimacy with your spouse, a desire for nice clothes, a desire for approval from someone in authority, etc.

WHY DID GOD CREATE ADAM TO HAVE NEEDS THAT ONLY GOD CAN MEET?

ASK Let the participants answer the title question before reading the paragraph.

ASK How does dependency on God's provision develop trust and intimacy?

As we see how faithful, accurate, and inexhaustible God is in meeting our needs, we learn to trust Him. We also learn to open our hearts to Him more as we believe the truth that He always wants the best for us and acts in our best interest.

GOD FASHIONED EVE (WOMAN)

ASK At that point, what did Adam need from Eve? Answer: Nothing.

Let the participants answer the question before reading the paragraph.

If the participants answer that Adam needed something from Eve, go back and revisit the sub-sections "Who Is Supposed To Meet Humanity's Needs?" and "Why Did God Create Adam To Have Needs That Only He Can Meet?"

EVE (WOMAN) WAS CREATED WITH WHAT INNER NEEDS?

ASK Let the participants answer this question before going through the content.

ASK What other needs might a woman have that are not listed here?

Listen for their unique perception of needs. This is not a time to correct the participants, but simply to discover their belief about needs.

ILLUSTRATION: MEN AND WOMEN CREATED WITH NEEDS

Review the guide to this illustration on page 154 of the *Living IN Jesus* Participant's Guide. The concept of God (illustrated by the triangle icon) was covered in Session 1. God creates out of who He is. He exists in relationship (Father, Son, Holy Spirit).

ADAM AND EVE WERE FREE TO GIFT DESIRES TO EACH OTHER

• • • • • • • • • • • • • • • • • • •

KEY POINT:
Because God met all of Adam's and Eve's needs, they were free to gift to each other their desires.

ASK **In what ways has God's life in you led you to meet the desires of others?**

If the participants do not have examples, share one of your own experiences.

ASK **How do we allow God to meet our needs?**

We allow God to meet our needs by believing He is enough and standing firm on biblical truths. God gives us faith. When we place our faith in God and His provision, we experience Him meeting our needs. There may be times when we do not feel like our needs are being met. In those times, we can ask God to affirm what He thinks about us and how He is providing for those needs.

TRANSFORM

After meeting together, the Transform questions allow the participants to process the session's truths on their own. Review the participants' answers with them at the beginning of the next session.

PRAYER
(10 min.)

Since relationship and intimacy with God involves conversation, we encourage you to incorporate both individual and group prayer into your study.

PURPOSE OF HUMANITY
Expressed Life

4

THEME

Humanity was designed to express God's life.

SUMMARY

God created man and woman to enjoy intimate fellowship with Him and to display His life (glorify God). Paul described the mechanics of glorifying God as the principle of the mind: 1) we receive a thought from the Spirit, 2) we process that thought, 3) we choose to submit our will to His direction, and 4) we carry out that action empowered by the Spirit. This process describes how to love God and, in turn, love ourselves and others. When we rest in God's provision and move only under His direction, we live from the inside out, accomplishing God's purpose for humanity.

TRANSFORM REVIEW

(10 min.)

1. On what have I based my ultimate worth and value? (performance, appearance, intelligence, possessions, career, status, other's approval, etc.)

This question prompts the participants to identify and acknowledge what they have relied upon as a source for worth and value.

2. What are my needs? Which needs are most important to me?

These questions encourage the participants to specifically identify personal needs and pinpoint those most important to them. The needs listed in the illustration on page 15 will help to answer this question.

3. Which attributes of God correspond to His ability to meet each need listed above?

This question helps the participants connect what God DOES (or has done) with WHO He is, leading to greater understanding of God and trust in Him.

4. In what ways have I seen God provide for my needs in the past?

This question brings the participants to acknowledge and thank God for His provision. God's provision may have been through Scripture, a song, a sermon, a testimony, a friend's act of kindness or encouragement, or an inner knowing in a time alone. Recalling God's past provision deepens our faith and dependency on Him.

> **TEACHING TIP:**
> Before beginning today's lesson, review the transform questions from Session 3: Needs of Humanity. The participant should have answered these alone before coming together for this session.

CONNECT   (10 min.)

 TEACHING TIP:
Remember to listen, not teach.

ASK **What has God revealed to you since we last met?**

This question opens discussion of any additional revelations not covered in the Transform review.

ASK **Name some examples of things built for a purpose where the design and function clearly express that purpose. (Example: a bridge)**

Other examples to consider: a chair, a cup, a light bulb, etc.

Possible follow-up questions: What does it mean to be designed? Does everything that has been designed have a purpose? These follow-up questions are meant to find out if the participants understand the relationship between design and purpose.

ASK **What was God's purpose in creating humanity?**

Listen for the participants' views of humanity's purpose. Is it behavior driven (doing something like serving, obeying, pleasing, or glorifying God) or relationship driven (being with God)?

ASK **What is God's purpose for your life?**

This question invites the participants to move from humanity's overall purpose to their personal purpose. If the participants have never thought about it and do not have an answer, then skip the next question.

ASK **In what ways are you fulfilling your purpose?**

Pay attention to how the participants personalize their answer from the third question.

 RENEW   (60 min.)

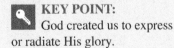

KEY POINT:
God created us to express or radiate His glory.

KEY POINT:
Glory is the visible expression or radiance of the beauty and character of God.

GOD CREATED HUMANITY FOR HIS GLORY

WHAT IS GLORY?

 ASK **Let the participants answer the title question before reading the paragraph.**

ASK How have you seen God's glory in creation?

Possible answers: The mountains display His majesty. A sunset displays His beauty. The complexity of the human body (or the universe) displays His wisdom.

ASK How have you seen God's glory in other Christians?

Possible answers: His love is displayed through forgiving an enemy (or someone difficult to love). His kindness is expressed through selfless acts of service or sacrifice. Supernatural peace is experienced in the midst of difficult times.

HOW DID ADAM AND EVE GLORIFY GOD?

ASK Let the participants answer the title question before reading the paragraph.

ASK Ask the questions in #4 of the Transform section (In what ways have you expressed the glory of God? What did it look like? What did it feel like?).

By addressing this question now, the participants answer it while it is relevant and later answer the same question alone with God.

WHAT ARE THE MECHANICS OF GLORIFYING GOD?

ASK Let the participants answer the title question before reading the paragraph.

ASK What enables you to glorify God?

Glorifying God can only be accomplished through the Holy Spirit (His presence - life, love, light, truth) in us. It cannot be achieved through fleshly effort or strength.

As we submit to the Holy Spirit, He animates our thoughts, emotions, choices, and behavior.

ASK How do you process your thoughts?

GLORIFYING GOD THROUGH LOVING RELATIONSHIPS

ASK Give the participants an opportunity to answer the question, "What is the greatest commandment?"

ASK How do we display the love of God?

If the participants miss the fact that unconditional love starts with God, emphasize that we must first receive His love and then share it with Him, ourselves, and others.

> **KEY POINT:**
> Adam and Eve manifested God's character, will, and life to each other by choosing to trust God, depend on His resources and operate under His direction.

> **KEY POINT:**
> The mechanics of glorifying God include: 1) receiving a thought from the Spirit, 2) processing that thought, 3) choosing to submit our will to His direction, and 4) carrying out that action empowered by the Spirit.

> **KEY POINT:**
> God wants us to receive His love and then share it with Him, ourselves, and others.

ILLUSTRATION: THE MECHANICS OF GLORIFYING GOD

Review the guide to this illustration on page 155 of the *Living IN Jesus* Participant's Guide. The left side of diagram was covered in Session 1 (Concept of God)
and Session 3 (Needs of Humanity).

TRANSFORM

After meeting together, the Transform questions allow the participants to process
the session's truths on their own. Review the participants' answers with them at
the beginning of the next session.

PRAYER   (10 min.)

Since relationship and intimacy with God involves conversation, we encourage
you to incorporate both individual and group prayer into your study.

THE TWO TREES
Life and Death

5

THEME

The two trees in the middle of Eden represent a choice between life and death.

SUMMARY

The two trees in the middle of the Garden of Eden represent a choice between two systems for living. The tree of life represents an option to trust God which leads to meaning, purpose, and fulfillment. The tree of the knowledge of good and evil represents an option to rely on perception, experience, and self-reasoning apart from God, resulting in death.

> TRANSFORM REVIEW (10 min.)

1. In what ways have I seen creation glorify God?

This question encourages the participants to consider the expression of God's glory in His physical creation (e.g., God's majesty revealed in a mountain, His beauty displayed in a sunset, His immensity viewed through the stars.).

2. How has the glory of God, as seen in creation, impacted my life?

After the participants acknowledge God's creation, they can share how His glory affects them personally (e.g., seeing a majestic mountain strengthens my faith and changes my perspective by reminding me of His unchanging power).

3. In what ways have I seen the glory of God in another person?

The participants focus on the manifestation of God's character in other people (e.g., fruit of the Spirit, as listed in Galatians 5:22-23).

4. In what ways have I expressed the glory of God? What did it look like? What did it feel like?

The participants acknowledge both their behaviors and their emotions as they recognize how God is expressing Himself through them. The emotions may be pleasant or unpleasant (e.g., an unpleasant emotion may occur when you choose to sacrifice for another.). Affirm with the participants how you have seen them display God's life.

TEACHING TIP:
Before beginning today's lesson, review the transform questions from Session 4: Purpose of Humanity. The participant should have answered these alone before coming together for this session.

5. What will indicate to me and others that I am truly expressing God's life and nature?

A person truly expresses God's life when actions are done in love, with a pure heart, and from a sincere faith in God (1 Tim. 1:5). This expression produces peace and joy. These fruits come with a clean conscience; evidence of the fruits are the absence of doubt, insecurity, anxiousness, confusion, and fear (James 3:13-17).

6. Take some time to listen. What is the Holy Spirit telling me in this session?

This question is used frequently in the Transform sections of the Living IN Jesus study. Continually encourage the participants to listen to the Holy Spirit for further, specific illumination. The Holy Spirit will never tell us something that contradicts Scripture.

7. How will the Holy Spirit's revelation impact my beliefs, choices, and behaviors?

Encourage the participants to express how the Holy Spirit is directing them; then support them as they follow in obedience. Real transformation occurs as beliefs produce changed behaviors.

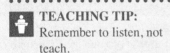

CONNECT   (10 min.)

TEACHING TIP:
Remember to listen, not teach.

ASK **What has God revealed to you since we last met?**

Discuss any additional revelations not covered in the Transform review.

ASK **How did God intend for Adam and Eve to realize a life of meaning, purpose, and fulfillment?**

Listen for the participants' views of God's purpose for Adam and Eve. Responses will give insight into their understanding of the previous session. If they don't know the answer, now might be a good time to review the mechanics of glorifying God from Session 4.

ASK **What other option was available to Adam and Eve?**

The participants explore alternate ways to invent meaning, find purpose and search for fulfillment apart from their Creator God.

ASK **When there are choices to be made, how do you decide what to do?**

The participants consider how they make decisions in life. If they do not mention asking God for His direction, a good follow-up question might be "Do you ever ask God for wisdom and direction in your decisions?"

ASK **What is the purpose of the tree of life and the tree of the knowledge of good and evil in the garden of Eden?**

Answers to this question lead you to the "Renew" section of this session. If they do not know anything about the "two trees," then explain each tree in more depth. If they are already familiar with the "two trees," then you will not need as much background explanation.

RENEW   (60 min.)

THE TWO TREES

ASK **Why do you think God put the tree of life and the tree of the knowledge of good and evil in the center of the garden?**

Possible answers: the importance of the choice, a more frequent opportunity to make a choice, easy access to the tree of life, etc.

LOVE IS A CHOICE

ASK **How is love connected to the freedom to choose?**

Without the ability to make a choice, there is no expression of love. God's love always involves choice. Without choice, actions have the appearance of love but are robotic and artificial.

ASK **What do you think it says about God that He told Adam and Eve they could eat from all the trees in the garden except for the tree of the knowledge of good and evil?**

Possible answers: God is generous, graceful, and protects. God made it easier on Adam and Eve by only making one tree forbidden. Etc.

A CHOICE BETWEEN TWO DISTINCT SYSTEMS

ASK **What makes something a choice?**

Without options, there is no choice.

TRUTH VS. THE LIE

ASK **What is truth?**

Truth is absolute reality. Truth must be both factually and logically correct. God's words are truth. Jesus is the living word and the truth (John 1:14; 14:6).

ASK **What lies have you encountered? How do they oppose the truth?**

The underlying lie mentioned in the Participant's Guide is that of self-sufficiency. Other lies may be: lies about God (e.g., "God is evil, uncaring, distant, or inca-

KEY POINT:
God placed two trees in the center of the garden, the tree of life and the tree of the knowledge of good and evil. Adam was told not to eat from the tree of knowledge of good and evil.

KEY POINT:
God's love is a conscious, free will decision to unconditionally act in the best interest of another.

KEY POINT:
The two trees represented two different systems of living with contrasting characteristics.

KEY POINT:
The tree of life symbolizes the truth. The tree of the knowledge of good and evil represents the lie of self-sufficiency.

pable."), lies about another person, or a situation (e.g., "I am less respected or unloved because that person does not show me respect or love."). This question brings the participants into awareness of lies in their current experience.

RECEIVING VS. ACHIEVING

ASK **What have you received from God?**

Possible answers: spiritual provision (salvation, new life, peace, forgiveness, etc.), material provision (food, clothing, or shelter), physical provision (health, talents, etc.), mental provisions (sanity, wisdom, intelligence), or relational provision (family and friends).

ASK **When have you tried to earn/achieve honor for yourself?**

GOD'S WISDOM VS. SELF-REASONING

ASK **Share a time you made a wise decision. What made it wise?**

If the participants do not have an answer, share from your own experience. This question connects the definition of wisdom and the process of attaining it to the participants' current experiences.

ASK **How did you obtain this (or any) wisdom?**

How do the participants understand the difference between God's wisdom and self-reasoning? If God is not mentioned as the primary source, explore the sources of the participants' wisdom. Attempt to connect the participants' source to the truth that God is the ultimate source of wisdom.

TRUST AND PEACE VS. DOUBT AND FEAR

ASK **What role does faith have in experiencing peace?**

Faith in God activates freedom from doubt and fear (Phil. 4:6-7).

ASK **Tell me about a time when you have been fearful and anxious. In whom or what were you placing your faith?**

Share your own experience first, then ask the participants for their experience.

FREEDOM VS. BONDAGE

ASK **In your life, what does it look like to live free?**

Possible areas of life to consider: job, family, social, church, etc.

KEY POINT: The tree of life represents a system where one receives from the hand of God. The tree of the knowledge of good and evil represents a system where one achieves or earns glory and honor for one's self.

KEY POINT: The tree of life symbolizes the wisdom of God. The tree of the knowledge of good and evil represents self-reasoning.

KEY POINT: The tree of life represents a choice to trust in God, resulting in His peace. The tree of the knowledge of good and evil represents doubt, resulting in fear.

KEY POINT: The tree of life represents freedom - God's freedom. The tree of the knowledge of good and evil represents slavery.

ASK **When you struggle with habitual sin, in what ways do you feel in bondage?**

Possible answers: Guilt, shame, and regret weigh me down. I become consumed with consequences. The person I hurt now dominates my mind and decisions.

 Caution: A believer is no longer a slave to sin (John 8:32, 36; Rom. 6:14; 8:2; Gal. 5:1; 1 Cor. 15:56-57). This truth will be covered in Session 8.

LIFE VS. DEATH

ASK **In what ways have you experienced God's life?**

Possible answers: I have received His wisdom about certain situations that has strengthened my faith. I have experienced His power to persevere through difficulties. I have received His comfort during painful times.

ILLUSTRATION: THE TWO TREES IN THE GARDEN

This illustration provides a summary of the session. It is possible to teach the session from this illustration, using the lists provided underneath each tree to compare and contrast the two systems of living.

- - - - - - - - - - - - - - - - - - - -
KEY POINT:
The tree of life represents God's life. The tree of the knowledge of good and evil represents death.

TRANSFORM

After meeting together, the Transform questions allow the participants to process the session's truths on their own. Review the participants' answers with them at the beginning of the next session.

PRAYER   (10 min.)

Since relationship and intimacy with God involves conversation, we encourage you to incorporate both individual and group prayer into your study.

CONSEQUENCES OF THE FALL
Loss of Life

THEME

Life was lost in humanity when Adam and Eve chose to sin.

SUMMARY

As a consequence of the Fall, Adam and Eve lost God's life, resulting in spiritual death and separation from God. Their physical bodies began to decay. They began to look for sources other than God to meet their needs. Their spiritual death produced a sin nature that changed their identity from children of God to children of Satan. The law of sin entered their bodies, and they developed coping mechanisms to try to meet their needs in the flesh. Adam's and Eve's fallen (condemned) condition has been passed down to all humanity.

TRANSFORM REVIEW
(10 min.)

1. What does a life of meaning, purpose, and fulfillment look like to me?

If the participants will share, you will learn how the world (fleshly/self-centered view) has influenced their belief systems, or how the Spirit (heavenly/God-centered view) is renewing their beliefs. Possible follow-up question: In what ways has your view of life's meaning, purpose and fulfillment changed over the course of your life?

2. Which characteristic of the tree of life encourages me most? Why?

The participants are encouraged to both review and make personal application of the truths included in this session. Since the Holy Spirit enlightens us individually through Scripture (John 14:26), answers will vary. As the Spirit prompts you, affirm and encourage the participants that they have been hearing from the Holy Spirit.

3. When faced with a problem, from which tree / system do I tend to operate? Why is that?

As the participants answer, be careful not to pass judgment or shame them. Because belief drives behavior, getting to the "why" behind what they do is important. If they admit to operating mostly from the "tree of the knowledge of good and evil," then the follow-up "why" question becomes very valuable. Judgment or shame can shut a person down, and consequently they will not feel safe enough to dig into the "why" with you. If needed, remind the participants of Romans 8:1 – "There is therefore now no condemnation for those in Christ Jesus." Once they discover the false belief behind their behavior, their behavior will change as they start walking in the truth.

TEACHING TIP:
Before beginning today's lesson, review the transform questions from Session 5: The Two Trees. The participant should have answered these alone before coming together for this session.

4. In what ways have I operated from the tree of the knowledge of good and evil? What were the results?

Responses allow the participants to reflect on the consequences caused by their sinful behaviors.

5. When in my life have I been fearful? What role did doubt play in that fear?

This question encourages the participants to associate beliefs with actions and feelings.

6. Take some time to listen. What is the Holy Spirit telling me in this session?

This question is used frequently in the Transform sections of the *Living IN Jesus* study. Continually encourage the participants to listen to the Holy Spirit for further, specific illumination. The Holy Spirit will never tell us something that contradicts Scripture.

7. How will the Holy Spirit's revelation impact my beliefs, choices, and behaviors?

Encourage the participants to express how the Holy Spirit is directing them; then support them as they follow in obedience. Real transformation occurs as beliefs produce changed behaviors.

 CONNECT   (10 min.)

TEACHING TIP:
Remember to listen, not teach.

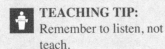 **What has God revealed to you since we last met?**

Discuss any additional revelations not covered in the Transform review.

ASK **What is the difference between life and death?**

Listen for the participants' concept of life and death. If needed, use this clarifying question: "What does it mean to be alive?"

ASK **What does it mean to be separated from God?**

Listen for the participants' particular viewpoint of separation. A suggested follow-up question is: "Can a person be separated from a God who is present everywhere?"

ASK **What happened to humanity when Adam and Eve chose to eat from the tree of the knowledge of good and evil?**

Probe the participants' concept of consequences.

RENEW

(60 min.)

THE FALL OF HUMANITY

ASK **What do you think Satan was trying to accomplish by deceiving Eve?**

This question encourages the exploration of Satan's intentions. Satan is separated from God and wants everyone to be separated from God as well.

KEY POINT:
Satan used deception to achieve his goal to get Adam and Eve to eat from the tree of the knowledge of good and evil.

LIFE LEFT ADAM AND EVE - HUMANITY DIED

ASK **In what way did Adam and Eve die on the day they ate from the tree of the knowledge of good and evil?**

Adam and Eve died spiritually because they were disconnected from the spiritual life of God.

KEY POINT:
When the Holy Spirit left Adam and Eve, they died spiritually.

ADAM AND EVE WERE SEPARATED FROM GOD

ASK **What led Adam and Eve to hide from God?**

Adam told God they were afraid. Doubting God produced fear. They may have doubted God's unconditional love, mercy, and goodness.

Follow-up question: What were they afraid of? Possible answers: God's disappointment, judgment, or wrath; punishment; their nakedness exposed; shame; etc.

ASK **Imagine being Adam or Eve in that moment. In what ways would your perception of God or yourself change?**

The participants may answer in terms of emotions, thoughts/beliefs, or behaviors.

KEY POINT:
Adam and Eve separated themselves from God by believing a lie and then sinning.

ILLUSTRATION: DEATH IS THE ABSENCE OF LIFE

This illustration builds on the analogy of the light bulb first introduced in the margin on page 20 of the participant's guide. After the fall, Adam and Eve were like the darkened bulb. They were cut off from the spiritual life of God, illustrated by the absence of the Holy Spirit. When the "light" of the Holy Spirit left, they became "darkened" in their understanding (Eph. 4:18). The broken filament indicates their changed nature which became bent towards sin and disobedience.

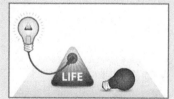

KEY POINT:
Adam and Eve's identity changed from being children of God (saints), to being children of the devil (sinners).

KEY POINT:
Cut off from God's life, Adam and Eve changed from living souls to souls that merely existed.

KEY POINT:
Instead of depending on God to meet their needs, Adam and Eve now attempted to meet every need through their own power and resources.

KEY POINT:
As a result of Adam's and Eve's spiritual death, the law of sin entered their physical bodies. Today, indwelling sin pulls us to gratify the sinful desires of the flesh.

KEY POINT:
Due to the Fall, the human body became subject to disease (the contamination of sin) and the process of decay and death.

KEY POINT:
After Adam and Eve lost life, they developed coping mechanisms to meet their own needs. These repeated coping mechanisms became habit patterns referred to as "the flesh."

IDENTITY CHANGED

ASK **Were Adam and Eve still considered children of God?**

Adam and Eve were still offspring of God in the sense that He physically created them, but God was not the source of their newly fallen nature. Identity comes from nature, not physical origin.

SOUL MERELY EXISTED

ASK **What is the evidence that a soul is merely existing?**

The evidence is an inner restlessness that manifests itself in fleshly behavior (Gal. 5:19-21 - anger, strife, jealousy, immorality, etc.).

NEEDS NO LONGER MET

ASK **What do you suppose were some of Adam's and Eve's deepest needs that now went unmet?**

Possible answers: love, acceptance, respect, significance, adequacy, peace, worth, relationship, etc. After the participants share their responses, review Session 3 and recall awareness of those unmet needs.

LAW (PRINCIPLE) OF SIN ENTERED

ASK **What are some ways your physical body increases the attraction to sin?**

Possible answers: We see attractive images with our eyes. We hear deceptions with our ears. We touch or sense another's touch. All of these ways arouse fleshly lust.

BODIES BEGAN TO DECAY

ASK **Have you or someone you know suffered from a debilitating disease? What effect did that have on your thoughts and emotions?**

Possible answers: reminds us of our frailty, leads to a longing for our new bodies, grieves us due to the loss and separation of loved ones, leads to a sense of hopelessness and powerlessness, etc.

PROGRAMMED FLESH DEVELOPED

 Teaching Tip: Briefly introduce the concept of programmed flesh here. Keep in mind this topic will be covered conceptually in Session 7 and with personal discovery and application in Session 15.

ILLUSTRATION: HUMANITY AFTER THE FALL

Review the guide to this illustration on page 156 of the *Living IN Jesus* Participant's Guide. This illustration is first introduced and explained in Session 2, pg.9. The focus here is to illustrate the effects of the fall on humanity.

CONDEMNED

ASK **What is condemnation? What does it feel like to be under condemnation?**

Condemnation means judged unfit, pronounced guilty, declared wrong or evil (e.g., A condemned building is a building marked for destruction.). Condemnation works against the need to be worthwhile. One who feels condemned can experience shame and a feeling of deserved, impending doom.

KEY POINT:
Adam and Eve stood condemned and lived under judgment because they were guilty of sinning against God.

ALL HUMANITY AFFECTED

ASK **How many times does a person have to sin before they become a sinner?**

Since everyone is born with the identity of a sinner (Rom. 5:19a), the answer is zero. People sin because they were born sinners.

KEY POINT:
Because the entire human race was in Adam and Eve when they sinned, all humanity has inherited their fallen condition.

ILLUSTRATION: HUMANITY DIED IN ADAM

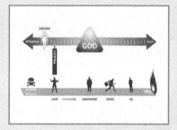

Review the guide to this illustration on page 157 of the *Living IN Jesus* Participant's Guide.

ASK **If your grandfather died before your father was born, where would you be today?**

You would not be alive. You would have died with your grandfather because you were still "in" your grandfather. In the same sense, the whole human race was "in" Adam when he died. Therefore, in Adam we all died (Rom. 5:17-18).

A BROKEN SYSTEM OF EXISTING EMERGES

Note: This sub-section is a quick review of Session 5.

ASK **How have you seen the "quality of your existence" depend on your choices?**

This question is not intended to shame the participants or try to expose any regrets. Share your experiences and tell how your choices have either led to desirable results or unpleasant outcomes.

KEY POINT:
After the fall, Adam and Eve no longer depended on God for life. Instead, the quality of their existence now depended on the outcome of their choices.

TRANSFORM

After meeting together, the Transform questions allow the participants to process the session's truths on their own. Review the participants' answers with them at the beginning of the next session.

PRAYER   (10 min.)

Since relationship and intimacy with God involves conversation, we encourage you to incorporate both individual and group prayer into your study.

DEVELOPMENT OF FLESH
Counterfeit Life

THEME

Flesh patterns are a counterfeit of God's true life.

SUMMARY

Born with a nature that is hostile toward God's love, acceptance, and value, everyone develops ways (flesh patterns) to make life work and meet their own needs apart from God. Whether confidence based or shame based, all flesh patterns result from false beliefs which lead to self-effort and futility.

TRANSFORM REVIEW   (10 min.)

1. What was my life like before receiving God's salvation?

The participants consider the contrast between their lives now and what life was like before they came to know Christ. If needed, help the participants key in on attitudes, passions and values.

2. What are my thoughts when I feel dead or empty?

The participants contemplate the connection between their thoughts and their feelings. This understanding will encourage them to start using emotions as a tool to discover true beliefs. (This concept is covered in more detail in Session 14.)

3. At what times in my life have I felt shame and condemnation?

The participants recall events that produced shame and condemnation. Those memories do not have to involve big events. Good follow-up questions may be: Why did you feel shame and/or condemnation at that time? Where do feelings of shame and condemnation come from?

4. How does knowing the consequences of the Fall change the way I see others who are not Christians?

Understanding the consequences of the Fall upon humanity, we will hopefully be more sensitive to the unbelievers' need for Christ. This question connects Session 6 to the reason unbelievers think and behave the way they do. (Session 6 will help the participants realize that unbelievers sin because they are dead to God.) We should not expect to see Godly behavior from people who do not contain God's life. The most natural and normal behavior for sinners is to operate by the law of sin and death.

TEACHING TIP:
Before beginning today's lesson, review the transform questions from Session 6: Consequences of the Fall. The participant should have answered these alone before coming together for this session.

5. Take some time to listen. What is the Holy Spirit telling me in this session?

This question is used frequently in the Transform sections of the *Living IN Jesus* study. Continually encourage the participants to listen to the Holy Spirit for further, specific illumination. The Holy Spirit will never tell us something that contradicts Scripture.

6. How will the Holy Spirit's revelation impact my beliefs, choices, and behaviors?

Encourage the participants to express how the Holy Spirit is directing them; then support them as they follow in obedience. Real transformation occurs when beliefs correspond to changed behaviors.

 CONNECT   (10 min.)

 TEACHING TIP:
Remember to listen, not teach.

ASK **What has God revealed to you since we last met?**

This question opens discussion of any additional revelations not covered in the Transform review.

ASK **What kind of things do people do to meet their needs for worth, love, respect, and acceptance?**

Listen for the participants' understanding of fleshly motives in themselves and others.

ASK **What patterns or habits develop as people continue in these behaviors?**

Listen for the participants' understanding of the connection between individual behaviors and repetition. Possible answers: performing for acceptance, blaming others, withdrawing, skeptical attitudes, distrust of others, fighting, etc.

ASK **What does counterfeit mean to you?**

Listen for the participants' understanding of the word "counterfeit." A good follow-up question might be: What does a person try to gain from counterfeiting something such as money?

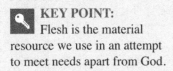 **RENEW**   (60 min.)

 KEY POINT:
Flesh is the material resource we use in an attempt to meet needs apart from God.

WHAT IS FLESH?

ASK **When you hear the word "flesh," what comes to mind? (This question is in the Participant's Guide.)**

Let the participants answer the question in the text first.

PROGRAMMED FLESH

ASK **What would it take to make you happy or satisfied in life?**

Possible answers: enough money, loving relationships, everything going my way, all expectations met, achievements, religious self-disciplines, etc.

ASK **What are some other examples of repeated behaviors that result in programmed flesh?**

Three full pages in Session 15 are labeled "Manifestations of the Flesh." A review of this list before your session gives some good examples of flesh patterns and how they are programmed.

ILLUSTRATION: HOW FLESH IS PROGRAMMED

Review the guide to this illustration on page 159 of the *Living IN Jesus* Participant's Guide. This is a continuation of the diagram in Session 6, pg. 36. The changes in this diagram will illustrate how flesh is programmed through re-thinking.

CAN OUR FLESH EVER FULLY MEET OUR INNER NEEDS?

ASK **What are some specific examples of futility? What are some negative consequences of operating out of the flesh?**

These questions can be answered out of personal experience or from stories in the Bible. One example of the destruction that comes from operating out of the flesh is mentioned in the margin. Read the story of Saul in 1 Samuel 13:6-14.

FLESH IS A CONTROLLER

ASK **In what ways do you try to control your life?**

Possible answers: schedule, finances, outcomes, relationships, etc. If the participants do not have an answer, you can share ways you have tried to control your life.

ASK **What needs are you trying to meet by controlling your life?**

Possible answers: security, acceptance, love, respect, significance, worth and value, etc.

KEY POINT:
When fleshly behaviors are continually repeated, they are programmed into our memory and can become default-responses or habit patterns.

KEY POINT:
Neither the physical things of this world, personal performance, nor other people on this earth will ever fully meet our needs.

KEY POINT:
Flesh strives to control the environment in order to produce success, worth, and security.

🔑 **KEY POINT:**
Usually family teaches us our first flesh patterns. We observe our parents' way of operating in the flesh and often adopt those measures for ourselves.

🔑 **KEY POINT:**
Confidence based flesh is a dependence on self, characterized by confidence in one's own abilities.

🔑 **KEY POINT:**
Shame based flesh is a dependence on self, characterized by a low view of one's self.

FLESH IS INHERITED

ASK **"1 Peter 1:18b says we inherited our futile way of life from our fore-fathers. What does that mean to you?" (This question is in the Participant's Guide.)**

Let the participants answer the question in the text first.

ASK **In what ways do you think your parents' behavior affected you?**

There is no correct answer. You may ask how they handled conflict or other personal habits. To give an example, share from your own experience how your flesh patterns were influenced by your parents.

CONFIDENCE BASED FLESH

ASK **What words or phrases in Philippians 3:4-6 indicate Paul had confidence based flesh?**

Paul says that if anyone was tempted to have confidence in the flesh, he would be that person. He had a high level of performance and accomplishments. It was "gain" for him. These things defined him and gave him meaning, value and purpose.

ILLUSTRATION: CONFIDENCE BASED FLESH

Review the guide to this illustration on page 160 of the *Living IN Jesus* Participant's Guide.

SHAME BASED FLESH

ASK **Go to the Transform section and ask the first part of question #4. Ask the participants to re-examine their answers on their own later.**

Typically, most people have a combination of both flesh types. After the participants respond, share some of your past flesh patterns and how they were developed.

ILLUSTRATION: SHAME BASED FLESH

Review the guide to this illustration on page 161 of the *Living IN Jesus* Participant's Guide.

FLESH IS UNIQUE TO EACH INDIVIDUAL

• • • • • • • • • • • • • • • • • • • •
KEY POINT:
Both confidence and shame based beliefs drive coping behaviors in attempts to meet inner needs.

ASK **What are some confidence based behaviors?**

Possible answers: boasting, judging others, arrogance, stubbornness, self-righteousness, haughtiness, excessive performance, talking down to others, etc. Let the participants answer in general, then ask:

ASK **What are some of your confidence based behaviors?**

Do not push this question if the participants are not ready to answer. People operating in the flesh do not like to be exposed until they surrender. If they do not seem to know, share some of your stories. This subject will be revisited in Session 15, "Identifying Our Flesh."

ASK **What are some shame based behaviors?**

Possible answers: putting oneself down, seeking compliments, isolating, harming oneself (cutting), having eating disorders, not accepting compliments, demeaning oneself in a humorous way, neglecting hygiene and appearance, etc. Let the participants answer in general, then ask:

ASK **What are some of your shame based behaviors?**

Do not push this question if the participants are not ready to answer. People who have shamed based flesh often hide or redirect the conversation when their flesh is exposed. If they do not seem to know or are reluctant to disclose their flesh patterns, then share some of yours. Your transparency will lead to a more intimate relationship and promote a safer atmosphere for the other person to share.

TRANSFORM

After meeting together, the Transform questions allow the participants to process the session's truths on their own. Review the participants' answers with them at the beginning of the next session.

PRAYER   (10 min.)

Since relationship and intimacy with God involves conversation, we encourage you to incorporate both individual and group prayer into your study.

GOD'S SOLUTION AND OUR RESPONSE
Provision for Life

THEME

Jesus is God's provision for redemption and restoration of Life to humanity.

SUMMARY

God, in the person of Jesus, has resolved the two problems that kept us from an intimate relationship with Him. He dealt with our sins (problem #1) when he became flesh and blood, fulfilling the Law, and paid the penalty for sin through the sacrifice of Himself. He removed our fallen and natural identity in Adam (problem #2) by crucifying our old self in Christ. Our response is to believe and receive God's provision for our salvation.

TRANSFORM REVIEW   (10 min.)

1. In what ways do I see these behaviors called "flesh" in people around me?

Noticing and acknowledging flesh behaviors in others should not be too difficult. It is often easier to notice the selfish patterns of others than to see how or when we are walking after the flesh.

2. What behaviors have I developed that came from frustration, anxiety, or discontent?

The participants should examine their own behaviors and connected emotions. These emotions can be a tool to lead us to fleshly behaviors. For this reason, it may be helpful for them to remember when they were frustrated and follow that to the resulting behaviors.

The key to discovering, disclosing, and repenting of flesh patterns is knowing who we are in Christ. We will visit flesh again in Session 15 following the sessions on what Jesus has done (to make us right), and the new identity He has given us as children of God. If the participants cannot or will not answer at this time, there is no need to press. This concept will be visited again. Hopefully, by Session 15 the participants will stand firm in their new identity.

3. What events or messages have shaped my belief system?

Responses provide a gentle start to the participants' discovery of their flesh and the false beliefs that drive fleshly behavior. (This question will be explored in depth in Session 15, "Identifying Our Flesh.")

TEACHING TIP: Before beginning today's lesson, review the transform questions from Session 7: Development of the Flesh. The participant should have answered these alone before coming together for this session.

4. Do I see myself exhibiting confidence based flesh, shame based flesh, or a combination of the two? What thoughts or behaviors demonstrate that in my life?

The participants analyze the primary category of flesh they have developed.

5. Take time to listen. What is the Holy Spirit telling me in this session?

This question is used frequently in the Transform sections of the *Living IN Jesus* study. Continually encourage the participants to listen to the Holy Spirit for further, specific illumination. The Holy Spirit will never tell us something that contradicts Scripture.

6. How will the Holy Spirit's revelation impact my beliefs, choices, and behaviors?

Encourage the participants to express how the Holy Spirit is directing them; then support them as they follow in obedience. Real transformation occurs when beliefs correspond to changed behaviors.

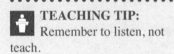 **CONNECT**   (10 min.)

 TEACHING TIP:
Remember to listen, not teach.

ASK   What has God revealed to you since we last met?

This question opens discussion of any additional revelations not covered in the Transform review.

ASK   What are the barriers to beginning a close, personal relationship with God?

The participants may answer "sin" or give examples of sins and may leave out the sinful nature. If they answer in this way, a good follow-up questions is: "What is another barrier?"

ASK   In what ways have people tried to remove these barriers?

How the participants answer this question will show you how much they have thought about salvation. A good follow-up question might be: "What does God want from humans before He enters a close relationship with them?"

ASK   Describe the Gospel of Jesus Christ in a few sentences.

Listen for the participants' understanding of how salvation involves both our sins and our old self. If a person only refers to the cleansing of sins and going to heaven, a good follow-up question might be: "Did anything else happen at salvation?" Remember to probe only the participants' understanding at this point rather than teaching.

ASK **What justifies you before God?**

Listen to confirm if the participant understands the concept of justification and its source. If the participants do not understand, a good follow-up question might be: "If God were to ask you why He should allow you to have a never-ending intimate relationship with Him, what would you say?"

RENEW

(60 min.)

TWO PROBLEMS WITH HUMANITY AFTER THE FALL

ASK **Look at the illustration, "Humanity After The Fall," in Session 6. What two problems keep humanity from intimate relationship with God?**

In the illustration from Session 6, the first problem (sins) is shown by the brick wall that is a barrier between mankind and God. This problem is the most obvious and noticeable of humanity's problems.

God designed us to be containers of His Spirit (life). The darkened, dead spirit (the old self) inside humanity is a second problem requiring a solution.

The correct answers are found in the rest of this session.

PROBLEM #1: OUR SINS

ASK **What is sin?**

Possible answers might include specific behaviors, thoughts, attitudes, or a general definition. The Greek word for sin is hamartia and means "missing the mark". The mark is God's design and purpose for humanity (Sessions 2-4).

PROBLEM #2: OUR OLD SELF

ASK **What is shame?**

A dictionary definition describes shame as a consciousness of being wrong, dishonorable, or improper. There is a difference between a condition and consciousness of shame. The difference is that one is a state of being shameful and the other is an emotion of shame.

GOD'S SOLUTION TO OUR PROBLEMS

ASK **How do we as humans try to fix these two problems (save ourselves)?**

Possible answers: Our good outweighs our bad. We go to church. We confess our sins for forgiveness. We are sincere. We remove God or remove the moral standard. Etc.

KEY POINT:
After Adam's sin, there were two barriers to humanity fulfilling God's design and purpose.

KEY POINT:
Sinful behavior makes humanity guilty and deserving of wrath from a just and holy God.

KEY POINT:
Humanity inherited an identity as unrighteous beings who are full of shame.

KEY POINT:
As a result of the cross of Christ, our two problems were dealt with and eradicated.

ASK **Why are these attempts incapable of solving our two problems?**

We are incapable of removing the obstacles because we are not God. We do not have the power, the resources, or the knowledge to save ourselves. The old self (sinful nature) cannot think or act beyond itself.

FORGIVEN, CLEANSED, RECONCILED AND JUSTIFIED

ASK **How many of your sins has God forgiven?**

God has forgiven ALL our sins. Good follow-up questions might be, "Has He forgiven the sins you committed today?" "Has He forgiven the sins you will commit tomorrow?"

ASK **How does knowing you are forgiven, cleansed, reconciled, and justified impact you?**

Possible areas to explore include the participants' view of God, self, others, relationships, life, obstacles, temptations, etc.

CRUCIFIED AND RESURRECTED WITH CHRIST

ASK **What do the words "crucified with Christ" in Galatians 2:20 imply?**

Let the participants answer the question in the first sentence before discussing the content.

ASK **How does knowing that your old self was crucified impact you?**

Possible areas to explore: the participants' views of God; their understanding of how God sees them; their view of self, others, relationships, life, obstacles, temptations; etc.

ILLUSTRATION: TWO SIDES OF THE CROSS

This illustration provides a summary of the session. It is possible to teach the session from this illustration, using the lists provided on both sides of the cross.

OUR RESPONSE TO GOD'S SOLUTION

ASK **What is saving faith?**

Faith is:

- allowing God to be God in our experience.
- our confident acceptance of Jesus' provision for the two problems that keep us from life with God.

KEY POINT:
Christ's shed blood secured our forgiveness, cleansed us from all sin, reconciled us to God, and justified us before God.

KEY POINT:
Christ's death, burial, and resurrection provided an avenue for the death of the old self (sin nature) and the creation of a new self in Christ.

KEY POINT:
God desires for all of us to believe in who He is and what He has done for us. He invites us to receive and embrace every gift that He has given us in Christ.

- taking Jesus at His word. He says He is God's Son and He came to give His life as a ransom for us (Mark 10:45; Acts 8:37).

- simply believing Jesus and then allowing Him to free us from sin and death.

TRANSFORM

After meeting together, the Transform questions allow the participants to process the session's truths on their own. Review the participants' answers with them at the beginning of the next session.

PRAYER   (10 min.)

Since relationship and intimacy with God involves conversation, we encourage you to incorporate both individual and group prayer into your study.

THE GREAT EXCHANGE
Restored Life

THEME

God exchanges His nature for our sin nature and restores His life to those who receive His gift.

SUMMARY

At the moment of salvation, we were made new creations indwelt by the Holy Spirit, and we entered into a new covenant with God characterized by abundant life. The old, sinful nature (old self) was exchanged for a new nature so we can naturally and uniquely express Christ's life in every action. We were given a full, spiritual inheritance with the guarantee that all needs will be met in Christ.

TRANSFORM REVIEW   (10 min.)

1. Have I ever believed and received God's provision for my salvation? If yes, how did that happen?

If the participants say, "No," ask them if they would like to make that decision now. If they say, "Yes," explore the basis of their belief. Are they trusting in works, church attendance, heritage, or in the finished work of Jesus Christ?

2. How does it impact me to know I do not have to pay my sin debt?

This question will give you as an equipper an understanding of how the participants view their sins. They will experience rest and freedom to the degree that they understand the magnitude of their sin debt.

3. In what ways does understanding my complete forgiveness change my experience of intimacy with God?

This question speaks to reconciliation of the relationship between the participants and God. People hesitate to have close or intimate fellowship with a person who is perceived as angry with them or holding a grudge. The more the participants understand the fullness of their justification, the more they will "draw near with confidence to the throne of grace" (Heb. 4:16).

4. What does it mean that my "old self" was crucified with Christ?

This question addresses identity. Many believers have the belief that they have two natures – one that wants to follow God and one that wants to sin. This question gives insight into the participants' views of what happened to their "old self" (sin nature) at the point of salvation.

TEACHING TIP:
Before beginning today's lesson, review the transform questions from Session 8: God's Solution and Our Response. The participant should have answered these alone before coming together for this session.

5. In what ways do I struggle with believing, receiving, and trusting God?

This question may shed light on misconceptions regarding the participants' concepts of God, how He meets their needs, and how they appropriate the life they have in Jesus.

 CONNECT (10 min.)

....
TEACHING TIP:
Remember to listen, not teach.

ASK What has God revealed to you since we last met?

This question opens discussion of any additional revelations not covered in the Transform review.

ASK What does it mean that every person is born with a sin nature?

Discern whether the participants connect nature to behavior or to the motivations and inner desires of the heart.

ASK In John 3:7 Jesus said, "You must be born again." What did He mean by "born again?"

Listen for the participants' understanding of spiritual birth.

ASK What is the role of the Holy Spirit in the believer?

Listen for the participants' understanding of the indwelling Holy Spirit as the restoration of the life of God in the believer.

A good follow-up question is: How is the Holy Spirit influencing you?

 RENEW (60 min.)

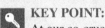
....
KEY POINT:
At our co-crucifixion with Christ, God removed the old sinful nature and gave us a new nature that is Christ's nature.

BECAME NEW CREATIONS

ASK If you are new creation in Christ, what happened to the old you?

This question is a way to reinforce the "newness" of the believer and test the recall of the participants. The answer from last session is that the old person is crucified. The old has been eradicated by the death of Jesus, paving the way for a new man to be raised to life.

ASK Do you believe that your true desires are righteous? If not, what is preventing you from believing?

Many Christians struggle to believe their new natural desires. Addressing the obstacles can help the participants distinguish between their experience (feeling) and the truth. This distinction will be covered in Session 14.

ASK How do you feel after you have sinned? What does that say about your true desires (nature)?

The participants' answers will reveal their true heart concerning temptation and sin. New creations do not want to sin.

ENTERED THE NEW COVENANT

ASK What is the purpose of a covenant?

Have the participants answer the question before reading the text.

OBTAINED AN ETERNAL INHERITANCE

ASK What is an inheritance?

Before you read the text of this sub-section, assess the participants' knowledge of inheritance and generate some discussion about this topic. An inheritance is something passed from one person to another after the death of the one who made the covenant or will.

ASK What other spiritual blessings has the believer inherited?

After reading this sub-section, the participants can use this question to explore other aspects of our inheritance in Christ, which are not mentioned in the Participant's Guide. This question explores the participants' understanding of their full inheritance. Possible answers: righteousness, victory over death, grace, freedom from sin, inner peace, etc.

INDWELT BY THE HOLY SPIRIT

ASK What is the purpose of being indwelt by the Holy Spirit?

Let the participants answer this question to reveal what they believe before reading the text.

ASK Tell me about a time when you sensed the Holy Spirit's power, help, or guidance. How did you know it was the Holy Spirit?

Share your own experience if it helps the participants connect these truths with their own experience.

SEALED BY THE HOLY SPIRIT

ASK What can a Christian do to unseal the Holy Spirit? Or, what can a Christian do to lose his or her salvation?

This question probes the participants' understanding of the security of the believer. The seal of the Holy Spirit is based on what God has done and what He continues to do, not on what we do (Phil. 1:6; 2 Tim. 2:13; Heb. 13:5; Jude 1:1).

KEY POINT: At the moment of salvation we entered a new covenant based on the finished work of Christ and not on our self-effort to be righteous.

KEY POINT: Everyone who is "in" Christ has received an inheritance that includes Christ's life, nature, power, and an eternal home in heaven.

KEY POINT: At the moment of salvation, the Holy Spirit enters believers causing them to come alive.

KEY POINT: When we place our faith and trust in Jesus Christ, the Father sends the Holy Spirit to live inside of us as a sign of His authority, our belonging, and the security that we will always live together with Him.

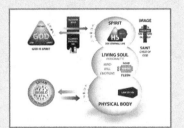

....

🔑 KEY POINT:
Through Christ's provision, God satisfies our deepest needs.

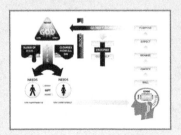

....

🔑 KEY POINT:
Through Christ, humanity's original purpose of containing and expressing God's life has been re-established.

ASK How does knowing the Holy Spirit will never leave you impact your relationship with God in your daily life? How does this knowledge help you face temptation or challenges?

The participants have the opportunity to connect a theological truth to their journey as a Christian. God's permanent presence is a perfect expression of His unconditional love.

ILLUSTRATION: LIFE RESTORED BY JESUS CHRIST

Review the guide to this illustration on page 163 of the *Living IN Jesus* Participant's Guide. This illustration is first introduced and explained in Session 2, pg.9. It is continued in Session 6, pg. 34. The focus here is on salvation and how a believer is made new and restored into relationship with God.

NEEDS MET IN CHRIST

ASK Do you feel loved by God? What if you do not feel loved by God?

The eternal proof of God's love is Jesus giving His life for us (John 15:13; Rom. 5:8). Feelings are indicators of our belief system but do not necessarily reveal truth. Just because we do not feel loved does not mean we are not loved. We do not need to pursue feelings, but truth. This topic will be covered in detail in Session 14, "The Believer's Battle."

ASK Over the last few weeks, in what ways have you experienced God meeting your needs?

If the participants struggle to answer, suggest examples of God's physical provision (air, food, clothing, etc.). Help the participants progress into emotional or inner needs (peace, calm, security, contentment, acceptance, belonging, etc.).

ILLUSTRATION: GOD'S PROVISION IN JESUS CHRIST

Review the guide to this illustration on page 164 of the *Living IN Jesus* Participant's Guide. This illustration is first introduced in Session 3, pg. 15. It is continued in Session 4, pg. 21, and shown as a broken system of existing in Session 6, pg. 36.

HUMANITY'S ORIGINAL PURPOSE RESTORED

ASK In what ways have you expressed God's life to others?

ASK How have you seen other Christians express God's life to you?

Both questions refer to the participants' experience in fulfilling their original purpose.

TRANSFORM

After meeting together, the Transform questions allow the participants to process the session's truths on their own. Review the participants' answers with them at the beginning of the next session.

PRAYER (10 min.)

Since relationship and intimacy with God involves conversation, we encourage you to incorporate both individual and group prayer into your study.

A NEW IDENTITY
Christ's Life

THEME

At salvation, a believer receives Christ's life and has a new identity as a fully accepted, righteous child of God.

SUMMARY

At salvation, we exchanged fathers - from Satan to God. Changing fathers produced a family exchange - from Adam's family to God's family. Our identity is now a dearly loved child of God who is righteous and fully accepted. As God's children we have an identity that is defined by who HE is, by what HE has done, and by HIS opinion of us.

TRANSFORM REVIEW   (10 min.)

1. Why does it bother me when I sin? What does that say about my true desires?

This question is crafted to help the participants focus on "who they are" instead of "what they do." If needed, help them make the connection between their disdain for sin and their identity in Christ. Remind them that saints hate sin even though they sometimes choose to sin. Help them understand that their truest desires are to avoid sin and consistently express righteousness.

2. In what ways have I experienced the presence of the Holy Spirit in me?

This question is designed to remind the participants of their times of intimacy with the Holy Spirit; they can build on that history to deepen the connection with Him as they go forward. Help the participants explore ways the Holy Spirit speaks to them. Assist them to note specifically what is going on in their thoughts and emotions. If they only mention dramatic, one-time events, a good follow-up question may be, "How do you experience the presence of the Holy Spirit in your daily walk?"

3. What does abundant life mean to me?

This question is designed to reveal the participants' understanding of abundant life. Do the participants' responses align with how the abundant life is presented in this session? Lead the participants to connect their understanding of abundant life to the truths taught in this session and to their answer to the previous question.

TEACHING TIP: Before beginning today's lesson, review the transform questions from Session 9: The Great Exchange. The participant should have answered these alone before coming together for this session.

4. What does it mean personally to be an entirely new being, a "new creation" made in the image of God?

This question should help the participants process their "newness." As an equipper, discern for an understanding that their newness is literal rather than just a label or the way God sees them.

5. What have I inherited in Christ? Make a list.

This question allows the participants to receive truths from the Holy Spirit and list the many aspects of their inheritance. This question emphasizes the past tense, "What HAVE I inherited…" Possible answers: Christ's life, Christ's nature, the Holy Spirit, citizenship in heaven, freedom from sin, righteousness, freedom from condemnation, a sound mind, the mind of Christ, a new identity, friendship with God, a spiritual family, every blessing in heavenly places, access to the Father, the fruit of the Spirit, etc.

 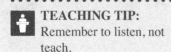 **CONNECT** (10 min.)

TEACHING TIP:
Remember to listen, not teach.

ASK **What has God revealed to you since we last met?**

Discuss any additional revelations not covered in the Transform review.

ASK **How do you identify yourself?**

Listen to discern the foundation of the participants' current identity.

ASK **What do people typically rely on to identify themselves?**

Possible answers: roles (such as mother or father), gender, race, heritage, career or job, physical appearance, social status, social media, etc.

ASK **In today's society, how do people change their identities? Why would they want a new identity?**

Possible answers to the first question: A wife changes her last name. A person enters a witness protection program. A person changes careers (re-invents himself or herself). A person has a sex change. A person changes titles (doctor's degree). Etc.

ASK **What does it feel like to go through an identity change?**

Listen to whether the participants can connect emotions to the underlying beliefs. If the participants struggle with answers, good follow-up questions may be: "How does a wife feel when she leaves her family and changes her name?" "How does a person feel when he or she gets laid off and becomes 'unemployed?'" "How do children feel when they grow up and leave the house?" "How does a person feel when he or she retires?"

ASK **How does family affect identity?**

Possible answers: last name, family role (husband, daughter, grandparent) family reputation, family appearance, etc.

RENEW   (60 min.)

FAMILY DETERMINES IDENTITY

ASK **What is your last name (surname or family name)?**

Get the participants to verbalize their last names.

ASK **How did you receive your last name?**

Family determines identity, not performance.

ASK **How do Christians typically identify themselves?**

Possible answers: their church/denomination; their discipline (strong, faithful, etc.); their theology; their works of service (choir member, deacon, volunteer, etc.); their spiritual giftings (teacher, evangelist, prophet, giver, etc.).

FULLY ACCEPTED

ASK **How accepted do you feel by God?**

The participants' answers to this question will reveal what they believe about their righteousness.

ASK **Under what conditions would God reject you?**

Their answers will reflect their perception. Lead them to realize NO conditions merit God's rejection once they become a child of God.

ASK **What more needs to be done to increase your righteousness?**

Nothing. Our righteousness is completely based on Christ's finished work on the cross. We will see in Session 13 how our behavior is being transformed to reflect our righteousness in Him. The key to our identity is characterized by the righteousness Christ has given us. Righteous behavior will follow as we believe and rest in our identity.

KEY POINT:
Just as people receive their physical identity from their physical father, so too, they receive their spiritual identity from their spiritual Father.

KEY POINT:
Through Jesus Christ, God made us fully acceptable by giving us His righteousness.

KEY POINT: The four points in the margin explain the process in which a Christian receives full righteousness from God - God offers, He reveals, we receive, and the Holy Spirit confirms.

KEY POINT: Since we have been given Christ's righteousness, we are as righteous as Jesus Christ.

KEY POINT: There are many aspects of our new identity as a child of God.

GOD'S CHILD

"He predestined us to adoption as sons through Jesus Christ to Himself, according to the kind intention of His will," Ephesians 1:5

INHERITING OUR RIGHTEOUS IDENTITY (IN MARGIN)

ASK   **What do you have to do to accept a gift from another person?**

Just hold out your hand and receive it. Receiving our righteousness is as simple as putting out our hands and humbly accepting God's gift.

HOW RIGHTEOUS ARE WE?

ASK   **Let the participants answer the title question and follow-up questions before reading the paragraph.**

ASPECTS OF OUR IDENTITY AS CHILDREN OF GOD

Teaching Tip: If you have time in your session, walk the participants through each one of the aspects by asking questions. However, if you do not have time, read together each aspect of our identity as a child of God; then take the participants to the Transform questions #1 and 2 of this session.

Our behavior is transformed as we renew our mind with the truth of who we are in Christ. These pages do not contain an exhaustive list of who we are in Christ, but they provide a great start. Suggest that participants place a copy of the list of these aspects of our identity as children of God where they will see regularly (e.g., bathroom mirror or refrigerator). When the enemy attacks with his lies, this visible reminder serves as a great way to continue believing the truth.

GOD'S CHILD

ASK   **What does it mean that you are God's child?**

Possible answers: wanted, chosen, safe, belong in the family, etc. The participants' answers help you understand their current awareness of what it means to be a child of God.

ASK   **Is it hard to believe you are a child of God? Why or why not?**

Lead the participants to move from focusing on circumstances, behavior, or feelings to the truth of God's Word. Review the sub-section "Fully Accepted."

ASK   **How does knowing you are a child of God affect your life?**

DEARLY LOVED

ASK Describe a time when you felt God's love.

ASK Describe a time when you did not feel God loved you.

Are the participants' answers to both questions based on circumstances? If so, lead them to anchor their belief and trust in God's unshakeable love demonstrated through Jesus' sacrifice. A good follow-up question might be, "What unchangeable truths convince you of God's great love?"

ASK How much does God love you? How do you know that?

God's love is measured by the ultimate sacrifice of Jesus and His present provision through the indwelling Holy Spirit (John 3:16; 15:13; Rom. 5:5-8; Gal. 2:20; Eph. 2:5; 1 John 4:9-11).

LOVED UNCONDITIONALLY

ASK Why do you think some people believe that God does not love them, or stopped loving them?

Possible answers: when bad things happen to them, their bad behavior, the loss of a loved one, etc.

ASK What condition would make God stop loving you or love you less?

Lead the participants to anchor their belief and trust on God's truth. Also refer to Session 1, "Concept of God," to review WHO God is. God cannot stop loving you because it is against His nature.

ASK How does knowing you are loved unconditionally affect your life?

FRIEND OF JESUS

ASK How does being a friend differ from being a slave?

ASK What does it mean to you to be Jesus' friend?

ASK How does a friend differ from an acquaintance?

For all of these questions, explore the different benefits and qualities of true friendship (e.g., loyalty, transparency, encouragement, acceptance, safety, support, dependability, etc.).

GOD'S PRECIOUS POSSESSION

ASK What words or phrases in this verse are meaningful to you?

ASK What part(s) of this verse do you have difficulty believing? Why?

DEARLY LOVED

"See how great a love the Father has bestowed on us, that we would be called children of God; and such we are." 1 John 3:1

LOVED UNCONDITIONALLY

"For I am convinced that neither death, nor life, nor angels, nor principalities, nor things present, nor things to come, nor powers, nor height, nor depth, nor any other created thing, will be able to separate us from the love of God, which is in Christ Jesus our Lord." Romans 8:38-39

FRIEND OF JESUS

"No longer do I call you slaves, for the slave does not know what his master is doing; but I have called you friends," John 15:15

GOD'S PRECIOUS POSSESSION

"But you are a chosen race, a royal priesthood, a holy nation, a people for God's own possession, so that you may proclaim the excellencies of Him who has called you out of darkness into His marvelous light;" 1 Peter 2:9

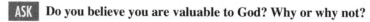

ASK Do you believe you are valuable to God? Why or why not?

ASK How does knowing you are valuable to God affect your life?

Understanding and believing our value to God meets our need for worth. It also helps us resist the temptation to earn value from our achievements and the acceptance of others.

BRIDE OF CHRIST

BRIDE OF CHRIST

"Husbands, love your wives, just as Christ also loved the church and gave Himself up for her, so that He might sanctify her, having cleansed her by the washing of water with the word, that He might present to Himself the church in all her glory, having no spot or wrinkle or any such thing; but that she would be holy and blameless." Ephesians 5:25-27

ASK Have you ever thought of yourself as the wife of Jesus? Why do you think Scriptures call those who believe in Jesus His bride?

A healthy marriage and the believers' union with Jesus are both characterized by unity, intimacy, love, sacrifice, protection, provision, faithfulness, submission, serving, etc.

ASK How does being Christ's bride make you feel?

Feelings of awkwardness may be experienced when we think of dysfunctional human marriages. Also, men may have difficulty thinking of themselves as a bride if they are only considering human or physical traits. Our marriage with Christ is a spiritual union.

GOD'S RESIDENCE

GOD'S RESIDENCE

"Or do you not know that your body is a temple of the Holy Spirit who is in you, whom you have from God, and that you are not your own?" 1 Corinthians 6:19

ASK What conclusions can you draw about your value in light of God's choice to take up residence in you?

This question leads the participants to acknowledge they are a container and expresser of God's life and the significant value of that truth.

ASK How does knowing God lives in you affect your life?

Possible answers: leads to honoring God with our bodies, helps us resist temptations, stabilizes us in difficulties, makes us conscience of His constant presence, etc.

BLAMELESS

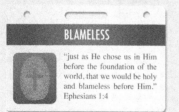

BLAMELESS

"just as He chose us in Him before the foundation of the world, that we would be holy and blameless before Him." Ephesians 1:4

ASK What does it mean to be blameless?

Possible answers: the theological definition (innocent of wrongdoing – Rom. 8:33), emotions involved in freedom from guilt, the effect of blamelessness on our thoughts and decisions, etc.

ASK How does knowing you are blameless affect your approach to God?

Hebrews 4:16 speaks to our confidence by saying, "let us boldly approach...."

NEW CREATION

ASK **Are you in Christ?**

If the participants say, "no", or are uncertain, go back to Session 8 and review the illustration, "Placed Spiritually into Christ." Those who are saved, are in Christ.

ASK **What old things have passed away?**

ASK **What new things have come?**

These first three questions allow the participants to acknowledge what God has made new (heart, spirit, nature) and what no longer exists (sin nature).

ASK **How does believing you are a new creation affect your life?**

Possible answers: Because our old self is dead, we do not see our nature as the problem anymore. It removes the shame associated with who we were (child of Satan/sinner). We walk in freedom which affects our decisions and behavior. Etc.

ADEQUATE

ASK **Describe some circumstances in your past where you have felt inadequate, incapable, or not enough.**

If the participants struggle to answer, share your own circumstances where you felt inadequate.

ASK **Where do feelings of inadequacy come from?**

Feelings of inadequacy come from false beliefs. The connection between feelings and beliefs will be addressed in Session, 14, "The Believer's Battle."

ASK **Does a person have to feel adequate in order to be adequate?**

This question leads the participants to move from feeling inadequate to trusting His adequacy.

ASK **How does possessing Christ's strength, ability, and adequacy encourage you?**

VICTORIOUS

ASK **What are some areas or situations where you feel defeated?**

ASK **What is keeping you from feeling victorious in these areas?**

Help the participants connect their negative feelings to lies they believe about their identity.

NEW CREATION

"Therefore if anyone is in Christ, he is a new creature; the old things passed away; behold, new things have come." 2 Corinthians 5:17

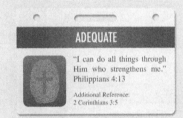

ADEQUATE

"I can do all things through Him who strengthens me." Philippians 4:13

Additional Reference: 2 Corinthians 3:5

VICTORIOUS

"But in all these things we overwhelmingly conquer through Him who loved us." Romans 8:37

ASK **Do you have to feel victorious to be victorious?**

Feelings are not good indicators of truth. Rather, feelings generally follow what we believe. Scripture says we "overwhelmingly conquer" (Rom. 8:37) and we "have overcome" (1 John 4:4). Therefore, whether we feel victorious or not, we ARE victorious.

ASK **What does victory look like in your life?**

Possible answer: fruit of the Spirit

NEVER ALONE

ASK **When do you feel alone or abandoned?**

This is an opportunity for you to remind the participant that no matter how alone they feel, God never leaves them.

ASK **How does knowing He is always with you affect you?**

Possible answers: comforts us, gives us boldness, gives us guidance, enhances intimate fellowship, etc.

PERFECTED, SANCTIFIED

ASK **Do you feel perfect? Why or why not?**

ASK **How does knowing you are perfected affect your life?**

GOD'S WORKMANSHIP

ASK **What does it mean to be God's workmanship?**

ASK **What words or phrases in Ephesians 2:10 encourage you? Why?**

ASK **What good works do you believe God has prepared for you to walk in?**

Possible answers: show God's love to my family, serve others in practical ways, show kindness. Other unique ways of expressing the fruit of the Spirit will be explored further in Session 12.

TRANSFORM

After meeting together, the Transform questions allow the participants to process the session's truths on their own. Review the participants' answers with them at the beginning of the next session.

PRAYER   (10 min.)

Since relationship and intimacy with God involves conversation, we encourage you to incorporate both individual and group prayer into your study.

INTIMACY WITH GOD
Fellowship with Life

THEME

We enjoy intimate fellowship with God as we talk to Him and listen to His loving voice.

SUMMARY

God desires a close relationship with His children because He is love. Our lives together with God are characterized by His leadership and our dependence. He leads us through love into greater intimacy with Him and empowers us, through the Holy Spirit, to follow Him. God fosters intimacy with us by speaking to us with His loving voice through the Holy Spirit. As we spend time with God in prayer and in the Scriptures, we learn to distinguish His voice from the voices of Satan and his demons. The Holy Spirit speaks to us directly in our minds by giving us thoughts, images, or impressions. He also communicates through the Scriptures, other people, and other means. Each of us is on a unique personal journey of life with God.

TRANSFORM REVIEW (10 min.)

1. Which aspect(s) of my new identity do I most believe and enjoy?

Encourage the participants to claim specific aspects of their identity in Christ.

2. What aspect(s) of my new identity do I have the most trouble believing?

If the participants are sincere, their answers will reveal areas where they have not fully accepted the truth. Encourage them in the truth of what God's word says about them.

3. What do "Aspects of Our Identity as Children of God" listed in this session (Session 10) say about God's opinion of me?

Reinforce some of these statements by affirming the participants with comments like "You are loved unconditionally," "You are adequate and never alone," etc.

4. What could keep me from embracing the truth of who I am (God's opinion of me)?

This question parallels question #2. The participants can explore further circumstances, lies, or emotions which influence them more than God's opinion of them in Scripture. A possible follow-up question: "What can you say to Father about this struggle?"

> **TEACHING TIP:**
> Before beginning today's lesson, review the transform questions from Session 10: A New Identity. The participant should have answered these alone before coming together for this session.

5. What will my life look like if I do not believe God has changed my identity?

The participants can identify their attitudes, emotions, behaviors (deeds of the flesh), and consequences of not embracing their true identity. When they understand the consequences of assuming a false identity, they are encouraged to stand firm in their true identity in Christ.

6. Take some time to listen. What is the Holy Spirit telling me in this session?

This question is used frequently in the Transform sections of the *Living IN Jesus* study. Continually encourage the participants to listen to the Holy Spirit for further, specific illumination. The Holy Spirit will never tell us something that contradicts Scripture.

7. How will the Holy Spirit's revelation impact my beliefs, choices, and behaviors?

Encourage the participants to express how the Holy Spirit is directing them; then support them as they follow in obedience. Real transformation occurs when beliefs correspond to changed behaviors.

 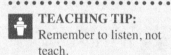 **CONNECT** (10 min.)

• • • • • • • • • • • • • • • • • • •

TEACHING TIP:
Remember to listen, not teach.

ASK **What has God revealed to you since we last met?**

Discuss any additional revelations not covered in the Transform review.

ASK **Have you heard the voice of the Holy Spirit? How did you hear Him? What did He say?**

Discern if the participants understand that we can receive direction and purpose directly through the Holy Spirit. If the participants cannot answer, provide your own examples.

ASK **In what ways has the Holy Spirit spoken to you in the past?**

Listen for how the participants uniquely identify and communicate with the Holy Spirit.

ASK **Why is there sometimes a struggle to hear from God?**

Possible answers: busyness, unaware of the possibility to communicate, unaware that God speaks to us, a poor concept of God, listening to deceptive voices, etc.

RENEW

(60 min.)

INTIMATE LIFE TOGETHER

ASK In what times do you sense God's presence?

Possible answers: church, struggles, traumatic events, special worship experiences, happy moments (birth of a child, graduation, anniversary, etc.), quiet moments (cup of coffee in the morning), etc.

ASK What do you enjoy doing with God?

The participants may give spiritual answers (worship at church, times reading the Bible or in prayer, quiet times, walking with Him moment-by-moment, etc.) or non-spiritual answers (talking to God on their commute, washing the dishes, cutting the grass, etc.). If the participants struggle with identifying routine and ordinary activities, share some you enjoy doing with God, or refer to those listed in the Participant's Guide.

ASK What words would you use to describe your intimacy with God?

ILLUSTRATION: SAFETY – TRUST – INTIMACY

ASK What is needed for you to reveal your deepest thoughts, fears, and failures to another person?

Ask this question before reading the text to the right of the illustration. If the participants struggle to answer, read the answers to the right of the illustration.

ASK Describe a relationship where you did not feel safe with the other person. What was your level of intimacy with that person?

The participants' experience can help them understand the connection between safety and intimacy more fully. If the participants struggle to answer, share an example from your life.

ASK What builds trust in a relationship?

Possible answers: faithfulness to someone over time, consistency in character, honesty, transparency, accountability, kindness, gentleness, etc.

ASK When do you find it most difficult to trust God?

The participants think about what restricts them from completely trusting God in every area of their lives.

KEY POINT:
God fully knows us and invites us to know Him.

KEY POINT:
Intimacy grows only on a foundation of trust, and trust develops within a safe relationship.

KEY POINT:
Our lives together with God are characterized by His leadership and our dependence.

KEY POINT:
The Holy Spirit leads us with love into greater intimacy with God and empowers us to follow Him.

KEY POINT:
As we spend intimate time with God in prayer and Bible study, we learn to distinguish His loving voice from Satan's voice.

A DEPENDENT RELATIONSHIP BASED ON TRUST

ASK In what areas of your life have you seen God's faithfulness and trustworthiness in action?

The participants' responses reinforce a healthy concept of God. If they cannot answer, share examples of God's faithfulness in your life.

ASK In what areas of your life have you struggled trusting God?

Possible answers: relationships, family, finances, education, vocation, health, spiritual life, etc.

GOD LEADS US BY HIS VOICE

ASK When you have heard God speak to you, what aspect of the fruit of the Spirit (love, joy, peace, patience, kindness, goodness, faithfulness, gentleness and control of self) did you experience?

ASK In what ways has your positive response to God's voice allowed you to hear Him even more clearly?

If the participants struggle to answer, share your experience. Emphasize that the Holy Spirit empowers us to lovingly respond to God's voice. Also, stress the importance of application.

GOD'S VOICE IS UNIQUE

ASK What aspects of God's character have you recognized when God speaks to you?

Possible responses: non-judgmental, loving, kind, gentle, graceful, merciful, considerate, persistent, patient, etc.

ILLUSTRATION: GOD'S VOICE VERSUS SATAN'S VOICE

ASK What distinguishing feature of God's voice encourages you the most?

Possible follow-up: "Describe when you heard this feature of His voice."

ASK What distinguishing feature of the enemy's voice do you hear in your thoughts?

Possible follow-up: Describe when you heard this feature of Satan's voice.

BY WHAT MEANS DOES THE HOLY SPIRIT COMMUNICATE TO US?

`ASK` **Let the participants answer the title question before reading the paragraph.**

THROUGH HIS VOICE IN OUR MINDS AND SPIRITS

`ASK` **What has been your experience with hearing or sensing the Holy Spirit's voice?**

Follow-up questions: How did you know this was the Holy Spirit? What was your reaction (your emotions and thoughts)? What convinced you that the Holy Spirit was speaking to you?

Refer to "God's Voice Vs. Satan's Voice" to help the participants discern the Holy Spirit's voice. If the participants struggle to remember an experience, share a time when you heard the Holy Spirit in your mind and spirit.

`ASK` **Describe a time when you experienced an "inner prompting" to serve others. How did you respond?**

Follow-up question: What emotions resulted from your obedience or disobedience?

THROUGH THE BIBLE

`ASK` **Describe a time when the Holy Spirit spoke to you through the Bible. What verse(s) did He speak through?**

`ASK` **Describe a time when you read the Bible and it was not impactful. What do you think was different than when you experienced God speaking to you?**

The participants explore and differentiate motivations for reading the Bible. Possible motivations: looking for a quick answer, trying to please God, obligation to read the Bible, seeking a blessing instead of seeking to know God, etc.

THROUGH OTHER PEOPLE

`ASK` **When has God used another Christian to comfort, encourage, teach, or exhort you? How did that experience minister to you?**

`ASK` **When has the Holy Spirit combined the Bible, other people, and His inner voice to speak to you?**

There are times when the Holy Spirit combines ways in which He communicates to us. For instance, we read a passage from the Bible and the Holy Spirit reveals a new or deeper truth to us. Later, another Christian speaks that very same truth to us as a confirmation.

KEY POINT:
The Holy Spirit uses many different means to communicate to us; but He will never take away from, add to, or contradict the completed Scriptures.

KEY POINT:
The Holy Spirit impacts our spirits and speaks truth into our minds. This aligns with God's written Word and leads to peace, comfort, and assurance.

KEY POINT:
As we read the Bible, the Holy Spirit highlights specific truths, instructions, or promises applicable to our current situation or struggles.

KEY POINT:
The Holy Spirit dwells in the hearts of believers and moves them to encourage, comfort, and exhort others.

····················
KEY POINT:
The Holy Spirit can speak through other means such as creation, dreams and visions, and angels.

····················
KEY POINT:
Whichever way God may communicate, each of us is on a unique, personal journey of intimacy with Him.

THROUGH OTHER MEANS

ASK **Has the Holy Spirit spoken to you through one of these other means?**

Ask them to describe their experiences. If the participants struggle with an answer, share one of your experiences.

ASK **What does God say to you through a rainbow?**

The rainbow is God's promise to humanity that He will never again destroy the earth by water (Gen. 9:13-17). Other possible answers: God is beautiful, creative, sovereign, faithful, etc.

A UNIQUE JOURNEY

ASK **Explain when another Christian's testimony about hearing from God discouraged you. What were you tempted to believe about yourself?**

ASK **What are some possible results if we compare ourselves to other's experiences with God?**

Possible answers: try hard to please God and others, devalue ourselves, forget how much we are loved by God, avoid intimacy with God and others, discard what we have received from God, stop sharing our experiences with others, exaggerate our experiences, etc.

ASK **What truths will help you genuinely enjoy how God speaks to others even if that is different from your own experience?**

Possible answers: I am unique in Christ. The enemy is tempting me to compare my experiences with others. I am God's child (i.e., complete, unconditionally loved, extremely valuable, etc.). Etc.

 **TRANSFORM**

After meeting together, the Transform questions allow the participants to process the session's truths on their own. Review the participants' answers with them at the beginning of the next session.

 PRAYER   (10 min.)

Since relationship and intimacy with God involves conversation, we encourage you to incorporate both individual and group prayer into your study.

EXPRESSIONS OF HIS LIFE
Displaying Life

THEME

God desires each new believer to "bear much fruit" as a beautiful display of His life.

SUMMARY

God designed us to uniquely express Christ's life. The Bible calls this expression "bearing fruit." Christ's life in each of us is our life. It flows from us naturally and spontaneously as we submit our will to His. Every believer is endowed with unique talents, abilities, and spiritual gifts. These enable the believer to individually express Christ's life for the benefit and edification of Christ's body – the church. Our expression of Christ's life is most evident when we focus on the truth and enjoy intimacy with the Father.

TRANSFORM REVIEW   (10 min.)

1. Why do I sometimes struggle with hearing God?

The participants should identify the hindrances to personally listening to God. Here are some possible reasons to explore further: busyness, distractions, unaware of His presence, emotional state, believing lies about God, etc. The demonic uses these tactics to keep us from listening to God (Eph. 6:12).

2. Set apart time this week to listen to God. Ask Him what He wants to say to you. As you receive a thought or impression, test it with the following questions:

- How is it consistent with Scripture?

- How does it align with God's voice versus Satan's voice? (See "God's Voice Vs. Satan's Voice")

- Is it producing peace, comfort, and assurance or fear, doubt, and anxiety?

This exercise guides the participants through the practice of intentionally listening to God.

3. How will the Holy Spirit's revelation impact my beliefs, choices, and behaviors?

Encourage the participants to express how the Holy Spirit is directing them; then support them as they follow in obedience. Real transformation occurs when beliefs correspond to changed behaviors.

> **TEACHING TIP:**
> Before beginning today's lesson, review the transform questions from Session 11: Intimacy with God. The participant should have answered these alone before coming together for this session.

CONNECT   (10 min.)

 TEACHING TIP:
Remember to listen, not teach.

ASK **What has God revealed to you since we last met?**

Discuss any additional revelations not covered in the Transform review.

ASK **What do you think gives our Heavenly Father the most pleasure?**

The participants share their views of what God enjoys. A good follow-up question might be "Why do you think these things give Him pleasure?"

ASK **How does Christ express His life on the earth today?**

Listen for the participants' understanding that Jesus continues His life on earth through those who have believed.

ASK **What characteristics are most evident when His life is expressed?**

This session describes the fruit of the Spirit as characteristics of Christ's life expressed on the earth through us. This question probes the participants' understanding of what God's life looks like and also reveals what they think is significant.

ASK **How is the fruit of the Spirit produced in a believer's life?**

Listen for the participants' views of how a believer can express God's life. Another way to ask this question might be, "What or who is the source of those features?"

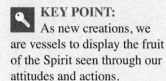 ## RENEW   (60 min.)

 KEY POINT:
As new creations, we are vessels to display the fruit of the Spirit seen through our attitudes and actions.

CREATED NEW TO BEAR FRUIT

ASK **Why did God originally create humanity?**

ASK **Why did God create us new in Christ?**

Make sure the participants remember the purpose of humanity (Session 4). The answer to both questions: so we would know Him intimately and display His life of love.

THE FRUIT OF THE SPIRIT

LOVE

ASK **What is love?**

ASK **Why do you think Scripture lists "love" first before all other expressions of the "fruit of the Spirit"?**

ASK **The Bible says even sinners can love those who love them. What is the difference between God's love and the world's love?**

This question contrasts the world's conditional love and God's unconditional love. Anyone can love under certain conditions; but if love does not originate from God, it is always conditional.

JOY

ASK **What is joy?**

ASK **What is the difference between joy and happiness?**

ASK **When have you seen a person experience joy even though their circumstances were not pleasant?**

Follow-up question: "When have you experienced joy even though your circumstances were not pleasant?"

PEACE

ASK **What is peace?**

ASK **How does God's peace guard someone in the midst of trials and adversity?**

God's peace is a calm assurance or inner rest based on His abiding presence and eternal perspective in the middle of our trials (2 Cor. 4:16-18).

ASK **Describe a time when you enjoyed God's peace in the middle of an adverse circumstance.**

PATIENCE

ASK **What is patience?**

ASK **What tries your patience? Describe a time when you were not patient.**

ASK **What does "slow to anger" mean to you?**

Possible answers: not easily offended, no buttons to push or chips on your shoulder, not quick-tempered, etc. When you are slow to anger you surrender unmet expectations of outcomes or another's behavior. You look to God to meet your needs, and your expectations are submitted to His provision and timing.

ASK **How does knowing patience is a fruit of the Spirit affect your approach to situations that try your patience?**

Patience is not self-generated; it comes as we realize that our new nature in Christ is patient. As we submit to Him, we are not easily offended and peacefully wait on others. You are offering the other person God's life.

KINDNESS

ASK What is kindness?

ASK Think of a time when someone showed you kindness. What made their actions kind?

A good follow-up question is, "How did it make you feel when you received kindness?" (This question expands the participants' awareness of kindness.)

ASK In what ways have you expressed kindness in your life lately?

If the participant does not have an example, give a personal example.

ASK What is the difference between God's kindness and the world's kindness?

A good way to discern the motivation is to discover what the person hopes for in the outcome. People who are led by the Spirit and believe God meets their needs, display an overflow of God's kindness. People walking after the flesh seek personal gain or recognition to meet their own needs.

GOODNESS / GENEROSITY

ASK What does goodness look like to you?

God's goodness is based on His character of love. God judges goodness based on motivation of the heart and the resulting behavior. The world's goodness is based on personal perception of behavior.

ASK Describe a time when you enjoyed the goodness of God.

ASK What is generosity?

ASK How is goodness connected to generosity?

ASK In what ways has God been generous to you?

Possible examples: salvation, a new identity, God's presence, eternal life, wisdom, provision for needs and desires, grace, everything we enjoy, etc.

ASK Describe a time when God led you to be generous? What was the impact on you and others?

ASK How does the idea of stewardship (as opposed to ownership) lead to intimacy with God?

Stewardship acknowledges the owner. Communication between the owner and steward is essential. The steward learns what the owner values, cheerfully agrees with those values, and manages His resources accordingly. Ownership does not require any communication or acknowledgement of anyone's values and input.

FAITHFULNESS

ASK What is faithfulness?

ASK 2 Timothy 2:13 says, "If we are faithless, He remains faithful, for He cannot deny Himself." How does this verse speak to you?

It is God's nature to be faithful.

ASK How has God shown His faithfulness to you?

ASK In what ways can you express faithfulness to God and others?

Possible answers: keep your word, be a doer of God's Word, remain close to someone in difficult times, go above and beyond what is expected, etc.

GENTLENESS

ASK What is gentleness?

ASK What does gentleness look like to you?

ASK Is gentleness or meekness valued in our modern world? Why or why not?

The answer may vary according to men's or women's perspectives. Help the participants understand that gentleness is not weakness, even though the world may think so.

ASK Give an example of how meekness serves as a strength in your daily relationships.

When meekness is displayed in relationships, trust and security develop.

SELF-CONTROL (CONTROL OF SELF)

ASK What is self-control?

ASK Give an illustration where you saw the fruit of self-control operating in the life of another believer.

Possible areas: when a person chooses not to say something unkind, when a person chooses not to eat or drink excessively, when a person chooses to bless an enemy and not curse them, etc.

ASK What is the difference between human self-control (willpower) and Spirit powered self-control?

Human self-control (will power) relies only on a person's own determination to avoid a wrong choice or a temptation (e.g., bite your tongue, count to ten, pop the rubber band on your wrist, etc.). Our role in self-control is to submit to the leading and power of the Holy Spirit (James 4:7).

KEY POINT:

🔑 Because the believer is connected to God, the fruit of the Spirit is produced naturally and spontaneously by the Holy Spirit.

ASK In what areas do you struggle with self-control?

Possible answers: words, emotional outbursts, eating, entertainment, sexual impulses, etc.

ASK How does knowing the Spirit provides you with self-control affect your life?

Possible answers: takes the pressure off to perform, more reliance on the Holy Spirit to empower godly desires, etc.

WHERE DOES THE ABILITY TO BEAR FRUIT ORIGINATE?

ASK What must take place first in people before they can bear the fruit of the Spirit?

They must be born again and have the Spirit of God inside them (Matt. 7:16-20; 12:33; John 13:35; Rom. 7:5).

ASK What is the difference between fruit generated by the Spirit and moral deeds produced by fleshly effort?

A good way to discern the motivation is to ask what is the person's intended outcome. People led by the Spirit believe God meets their needs and acts out of an overflow of God's kindness; people walking after the flesh seek personal gain or recognition to meet their own needs for worth and value.

ASK How have you tried to produce moral deeds by fleshly efforts? What were the results?

You may share your own experiences to help the participants understand the question and gain insight into their own behaviors and motivations.

ASK What does it mean to abide in Christ?

Listen for the participants' understanding of what it means to abide. 1 John 4:13 says to have the Holy Spirit is to abide. Abide means "to live," "remain," or "stay." All Christians, therefore, are always abiding in Christ. As a Christian believes their continual state of abiding and submits to the Holy Spirit, they will display His fruit.

WHO BENEFITS FROM FRUIT BEARING?

KEY POINT:

🔑 We bear the Spirit's fruit in order to bless and encourage others and spread God's life.

ASK Describe a time when you shared the Spirit's fruit with others. How did they respond? In what ways did they benefit?

Most answers will evoke positive responses and immediate benefit. Some people may respond negatively, but the immediate response does not determine benefit or harm. God – not us – ensures that others will benefit.

MAXIMIZING FRUIT PRODUCTION

ASK **What is the job of a gardener?**

The ultimate job or purpose of a gardener is to increase fruit production by cultivating and protecting the fruit trees or vines.

ASK **Scripture says that God is a farmer (vineyard caretaker) (John 15:1). In what ways is He like a man who cultivates and protects grape vines?**

This question probes the participants' understanding of the content in this sub-section.

ASK **Share some ways God maximized the expression of spiritual fruit through your life.**

KEY POINT:
God desires to produce fruit abundantly in our lives by cultivating us to better receive His truth and to submit to His leading.

TRANSFORM

After meeting together, the Transform questions allow the participants to process the session's truths on their own. Review the participants' answers with them at the beginning of the next session.

PRAYER (10 min.)

Since relationship and intimacy with God involves conversation, we encourage you to incorporate both individual and group prayer into your study.

GROWING IN GRACE AND KNOWLEDGE
Cultivating Life

THEME

We cultivate Christ's Life in us by pursuing greater intimacy with God.

SUMMARY

While our spiritual growth is caused by God, we can foster this growth through spiritual disciplines which include Bible study, worship, prayer, fasting, giving thanks, etc. These activities provide opportunities to deepen our intimacy with God. We do not engage in them in order to earn God's acceptance or to achieve righteousness through self-effort. Spiritual disciplines, when carried out under the direction of the Holy Spirit, become ways of enjoying His presence and a means of knowing Him more intimately.

TRANSFORM REVIEW   (10 min.)

1. What does my expression of Christ's life look like?

While answers will vary, they should all represent something Jesus did as He depended on the Father (loving, serving, praying, healing, acts of kindness, etc.) If needed, make the connection between the participants' personal, Spirit-led behaviors and the fruit of the Spirit.

2. Describe a recent situation where I bore fruit? Who benefited?

This question prompts recall of a recent, personal event in order to recognize the working and leading of the Spirit within believers. Encourage the participants to think about times where they have displayed love, joy, peace, patience, kindness, gentleness, goodness, faithfulness, and self-control. However, if a person thinks of all the times when they have failed, assure them there is no condemnation to those who are in Christ Jesus. Focus on their beliefs about God and who they are in Christ. Your encouragement will strengthen the participants' faith as they recognize how God has used them. The second question draws attention to the one(s) who benefited. A good follow-up question may be, "How did that that person (or those people) benefit?" In 2 Corinthians 13:5, Paul instructs us to test ourselves to see what we believe. Looking at the fruit coming out of our lives is a great way to test ourselves. Right believing results in right behavior.

3. What keeps me from expressing His life?

Believing lies about who God is and/or my identity in Christ will keep me from expressing God's life. We will discuss this in Session 14. How the participants respond allows you to discover their beliefs about the spiritual battle we all face.

TEACHING TIP:
Before beginning today's lesson, review the transform questions from Session 12: Expressions of His Life. The participant should have answered these alone before coming together for this session.

4. Take some time to listen. What is the Holy Spirit telling me in this session?

This question is used frequently in the Transform sections of the *Living IN Jesus* study. Continually encourage the participants to listen to the Holy Spirit for further, specific illumination. The Holy Spirit will never tell us something that contradicts Scripture.

5. How will the Holy Spirit's revelation impact my beliefs, choices, and behaviors?

Encourage the participants to express how the Holy Spirit is directing them; then support them as they follow in obedience. Real transformation occurs as beliefs produce changed behaviors.

 CONNECT (10 min.)

 TEACHING TIP:
Remember to listen, not teach.

ASK **What has God revealed to you since we last met?**

Discuss any additional revelations not covered in the Transform review.

ASK **What is spiritual growth?**

Listen for the participants' concept of spiritual growth. Does their answer focus largely on behavioral change, or do they also talk about change in thoughts, beliefs, and attitudes?

ASK **What causes spiritual growth?**

If the participants cannot answer the previous question, then they will not have an answer for this question. If they do respond, simply listen to their concepts of what causes or produces spiritual growth in a believer.

ASK **What motivates you to pray and read your Bible?**

Answers to this question reveal views of their own righteousness and what motivates their Bible reading. Some people read their Bible to earn God's favor. Such a response indicates they are trying to earn favor from God. A person may say, "I do not currently pray or read my Bible." A good follow-up statement might be, "Tell me more about that." (Make sure you make this statement in a tone of voice and facial expression that convey genuine interest rather than contempt and condemnation.)

ASK **What kind of things build intimacy with God?**

Responses give you insight into the level of intimacy between the participants and the Heavenly Father. Answers also reveal how they believe intimacy is developed. If this question completely stumps the participants, a good follow-up question might be, "What does intimacy mean?"

⟩ RENEW

WHAT IS SPIRITUAL GROWTH?

ASK **Let the participants answer the title question.**

ASK **What are the signs of spiritual growth in a person?**

Suggest the participants use examples of people they know. Possible answers: more consistent victory over temptation, showing more patience, resting in Christ's peace, experiencing freedom from fear, generous servanthood, forgiving others, growing awareness of God's constant presence, etc.

ASK **In what ways have your desires and behaviors changed since you were made new in Christ and given the Holy Spirit?**

Share your own examples if the participants cannot give an answer.

WHO CAUSES THE GROWTH?

ASK **Let the participants answer the title question.**

Do the participants believe that they cause the growth or do they know that God causes the maturing of every one of His children?

ASK **Identify times of growth in your life when you felt God's love. What was God doing inside of you during those times?**

Listen for what is going on in the participants' thoughts, emotions, and belief system.

HOW DO WE PURSUE INTIMACY WITH GOD?

ASK **Let the participants answer the title question.**

ASK **What does intimacy with God mean to you?**

ASK **What are some activities you do to foster intimacy with God?**

These activities might include the disciplines listed in the Participant's Guide, or they could be activities such as regular conversation with God in everyday life, writing (stories, poetry, articles, books, etc.), composing music, enjoying God's creation, etc.

ASK **Is it possible to implement spiritual disciplines in your life and not grow in intimacy with God? Why or why not?**

Growth is only achieved when we are led by the Holy Spirit and practice spiritual discipline as an opportunity to foster intimacy with God. If we rely on any moti-

---

KEY POINT:
Spiritual growth is the process of maturing in God's grace and knowledge so the life of Christ might be manifested externally in our every word and deed.

KEY POINT:
God alone works in us, causing us to grow. Our role is to pursue intimacy with God and submit to His leading.

KEY POINT:
Spiritual disciplines, when carried out under the direction of the Holy Spirit, are opportunities to foster intimacy with God.

vation or purpose that represents performance or attainment of God's favor, then growth in intimacy is not fostered.

BIBLE STUDY

ASK **What is one of your favorite passages in the Bible? Why are those verses meaningful to you?**

ASK **Describe a time when God used a passage in the Bible to impact you significantly in your growth as a Christian.**

If the participants have difficulty describing the impact, you might ask, "Did it comfort you? Guide you? Make you aware of God's character? Lead you to an understanding of truth?"

WORSHIP

ASK **What is the difference between superficial worship (going through the motions) and worshipping God from your heart?**

It is possible to speak or sing words of praise out loud to God when inwardly desires of the flesh have captured our affection.

ASK **Describe a meaningful time of worship in your past. What was going on in your thoughts and emotions?**

Worship is not limited to church services or group settings. Meaningful worship can happen anywhere or anytime (e.g., driving down the road, sitting on the beach, working on the job, etc.) as a response to God's truth spoken into our hearts.

PRAYER

ASK **Do you enjoy conversing with God? Why or why not?**

This question might reveal the participants' motivation for praying. Possible motives: religious obligation (checking the box), asking for answers and provision only, trying to gain more of God's acceptance, or enjoyment of His presence alone. God's Spirit supplies the joy in your conversation as you enjoy His presence and trust Him (Ps. 16:11; Gal. 5:22).

ASK **How do you talk to God?**

ASK **How does He speak to you?**

Prayer is a two-way conversation. It is not only making our thoughts known to God, but also being still and listening as He makes His thoughts known to us. Remind the participants that God's thoughts will always align with Scripture.

ASK **What obstacles or barriers keep you from conversing more with God?**

Some possible barriers could be doubt, busyness, pride, false concept of God, etc. All originate with Satan and his demons using the world system.

KEY POINT:
By spending time in God's word, we feed our minds truth so the Holy Spirit can renew our minds and, as a result, transform our behavior.

KEY POINT:
For a believer, worship is a continual expression of thanks and praise to God flowing from a heart of love.

KEY POINT:
Prayer is our continual, intimate conversation which involves both talking with and listening to God.

FASTING

ASK **Have you ever fasted? What was that like? What was the outcome?**

Listen for the participants' experience with fasting.

ASK **When fasting, why does the Bible say not to draw attention to ourselves?**

Fasting is not intended to be a means of earning favor from God or respect from others (i.e., fleshly activity with religious appearance).

GIVING THANKS

ASK **What are some gifts you have received from God?**

Answers will be unique to each person. Possible answers: talents, health, good mind, wisdom, practical provision, salvation, forgiveness, adoption into God's family, etc.

ASK **Describe a time when you thanked God in the midst of a difficult situation. How did that affect your attitude?**

OTHER DISCIPLINES

ASK **What are some other "spiritual disciplines" the Holy Spirit might urge us to engage in?**

Possible answers: serving, reflection, resting, silence, etc.

ASK **Why does God want us to get together with other children of God?**

The Bible pictures a believer both as a temple of the Holy Spirit and also as a collective "body" of Jesus (1 Cor. 12:12-27). We each make up an essential part of the "body" and are designed by God to work together to manifest His life in the world. One of the reasons God tells us to gather together regularly is to encourage one another and stir each other up to love and good works (Heb. 10:24-25). We are encouraged to teach and admonish one another in all wisdom (Col. 3:16). We are also instructed to exhort one another so we will not be hardened by the deceitfulness of sin (Heb. 3:13). As we enjoy Christ's life and express Him to one another, we each grow in intimacy with God.

ASK **Share when another believer really encouraged you. How did that impact your personal relationship with Jesus?**

ASK **Luke 5:16 tells us that Jesus would frequently slip away into the wilderness and spend time alone with His Heavenly Father. Why do you think He did that? What do you think they talked about during those times?**

ASK **Have you ever gotten away and spent extended time alone with God? If so, describe that experience.**

KEY POINT: Fasting is the act of denying ourselves something physical to focus our minds on God and the truth. Spirit-led fasting leads to greater dependence on God and deeper intimacy with Him.

KEY POINT: Thanksgiving is an expression of gratitude and an integral part of a healthy, intimate relationship with our generous God.

KEY POINT: The Holy Spirit will lead believers to engage in other spiritual activities that enhance intimacy.

TRANSFORM

After meeting together, the Transform questions allow the participants to process the session's truths on their own. Review the participants' answers with them at the beginning of the next session.

PRAYER   (10 min.)

Since relationship and intimacy with God involves conversation, we encourage you to incorporate both individual and group prayer into your study.

THE BELIEVER'S BATTLE
Reigning in Life

THEME

Reigning in life involves overcoming the enemy who battles us in our minds.

SUMMARY

Christ secured the victory once and for all at the cross, but He has not yet banished Satan and the forces of evil in this world. God made us new spiritually, but He left us temporarily in our dying bodies with a choice to live either from the inside out or from the outside in. God has not erased our memories; instead He asks and instructs us to consider ourselves dead to the old fleshly ways and alive to His life within us. The war is being waged each and every day in our minds. When we reject the lies, believe the truth, and move under the direction and power of the Holy Spirit, we walk in the victory that is ours in Christ.

TRANSFORM REVIEW (10 min.)

1. In what ways do I enjoy intimacy with God?

If the participants have no answer or do not enjoy intimacy with God, suggest they ask God how to recognize intimacy with Him or what inhibits that intimacy.

2. Think about a special time with God in prayer or Bible study. What made it special?

The participants consider how their interaction with God affected their life in the moment. Encourage them to describe in detail the experience.

3. As I spend intentional time fostering intimacy with God (Bible study, meditation, prayer, etc.), what have I noticed about my attitude regarding God? Myself? Other people? Life situations?

4. If I do not connect with other believers, how does that affect my growth?

The participants consider the importance of growing in community with others.

5. Take some time to listen. What is the Holy Spirit telling me in this session?

This question is used frequently in the Transform sections of the *Living IN Jesus* study. Continually encourage the participants to listen to the Holy Spirit for further, specific illumination. The Holy Spirit will never tell us something that contradicts Scripture.

> **TEACHING TIP:**
> Before beginning today's lesson, review the transform questions from Session 13: Growing in Grace and Knowledge. The participant should have answered these alone before coming together for this session.

6. How will the Holy Spirit's revelation impact my beliefs, choices, and behaviors?

Encourage the participants to express how the Holy Spirit is directing them; then support them as they follow in obedience. Real transformation occurs when beliefs correspond to changed behaviors.

CONNECT   (10 min.)

TEACHING TIP:
Remember to listen, not teach.

ASK **What has God revealed to you since we last met?**

Discuss any additional revelations not covered in the Transform review.

ASK **Where do your thoughts originate?**

This question focuses on the participants' understanding of thoughts and how they originate in the mind.

ASK **What is spiritual warfare?**

Discuss (do not teach) beliefs/opinions about spiritual warfare. Possible follow-up questions might be; "Is there a spiritual war?", "What struggles are there between good and evil?", "Who opposes God in the spiritual realm?", and "What do you think about demons?"

ASK **How do you know when you are under spiritual attack?**

Responses might include their thoughts, emotions, or behavior.

RENEW   (60 min.)

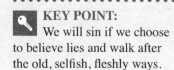
KEY POINT:
We will sin if we choose to believe lies and walk after the old, selfish, fleshly ways.

IF WE ARE NEW CREATIONS AND HAVE THE HOLY SPIRIT, WHY DO WE STILL SIN?

ASK **Let the participants answer the title question before reading the paragraph.**

ASK **Why does God not remove our memories and programmed flesh at the moment of salvation?**

God wants us to learn dependency on Him and expand our understanding of His power, goodness, and love. We grow in dependency and knowledge of Him through our struggles and spiritual warfare.

ARE WE REALLY AT WAR?

ASK Let the participants answer the title question before reading the paragraph.

ASK In what ways are you aware of this battle in your personal life?

This question (and sub-section) is designed to raise awareness of spiritual warfare. Use the participants' answers to guide you in how much detail to explore in this sub-section.

ASK What methods has Satan used to attack you?

Possible answers: temptation, discouraging thoughts, condemnation, false accusation, slander, racing thoughts, etc.

WHICH SIDE ARE WE ON?

ASK Let the participants answer the title question before reading the paragraph.

ASK What determines whether we are on God's side (in His family) or on Satan's side (in Satan's family)?

We were born into Satan's family. When we accept Jesus as our Lord and Savior, we are made new and adopted into the family of God as a gift. Neither sinning nor trying to act righteous determines or changes our family status.

WHERE DO THE BATTLES TAKE PLACE?

ASK Let the participants answer the title question before reading the paragraph.

ASK Who is presently working (or fighting) against you? How do their behaviors make them appear to be your enemy? Who is your real enemy?

Use this question to reinforce the truth that neither ourselves nor others are our adversaries (Eph. 6:12). Satan and his demonic forces are the enemy.

ASK What lies that brought conflict into your relationships have you believed?

In Session 15, the participants will be asked to expose the lies which they believed and which have resulted in conflict and frustration. If the participants have trouble connecting lies to conflict in their experience, share examples from your life.

KEY POINT:
Satan actively works to thwart the works of God. He desires the death and destruction of all humanity.

KEY POINT:
At the moment of salvation, we leave Satan's family and join God's family. While we are on this earth, battles remain for us to fight even though God has won the war.

KEY POINT:
In our minds, God's truths mix with lies from the world and the demonic; this results in a battle for our beliefs and obedience.

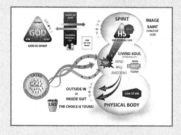

••••••••••••••••••••
🔑 **KEY POINT:**
Victory over Satan is experienced through knowing and believing truth and then choosing to act under the direction of the Spirit.

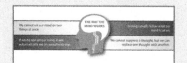

ILLUSTRATION: THE BATTLE FOR THE MIND

Review the guide to this illustration on page 165 of the *Living IN Jesus* Participant's Guide. This illustration, first introduced in Session 2, p. 9, shows the design of man. It is continued in Session 6, p. 34, to show man after the fall. Finally, in Session 9, p. 55, this diagram is developed to show how God has restored us.

WHAT DOES VICTORY OVER SATAN LOOK LIKE?

ASK **Let the participants answer the title question before reading the paragraph.**

ASK **What are the consequences of succumbing to Satan's schemes?**

When yielding to his schemes, we make ourselves vulnerable to further accusations (e.g., Once we sin, Satan may tell us we are terrible failures as Christians.) As we believe Satan's lies, we will walk after the flesh. Possible consequences: destroyed relationships, emotional struggles (doubt, worry, fear) due to insecurity, financial loss, etc.

ASK **Share when you experienced victory over a temptation. What were you believing about God, yourself, and your situation? What lie did the enemy use to tempt you?**

Use an example in your life if the participants struggle to answer.

ILLUSTRATION: TARGETING LIES WITH THE TRUTH

We can use our emotions to target lies we are believing in the same way a person uses a scope on a gun to find a target.

ASK **What are some of the lies (in the center [scope] of the illustration) you have felt before? What truths (bullets) would you use to destroy the lies?**

If the participants have never put 2 Corinthians 10:5 into practice, talk them through the process: recognize lies, take them captive to the obedience of Christ, and replace the lies with the truth from God (Jude 9).

ILLUSTRATION: THE WAY THE MIND WORKS

ASK **What happens to our emotions and attitudes when we believe the truth and live from it?**

Listen for aspects of the fruit of the Spirit. Several Biblical examples of faith resulting in peace are Elisha and his servant (2 Kings 6:14-17), the stoning of Stephen (Acts 7:54-60), Paul and his shipwreck experience (Acts 27:23-25; 28:4-6), and Paul in prison (Acts 16:22-25).

WHAT ARE SOME COMMON DECEPTIONS ABOUT VICTORY?

ASK **In what ways have you attempted to overcome sin? How well did they work?**

Listen for indications of fleshly attempts. Any attempt to overcome sin using fleshly resources will fail. (Refer to "Manifestations of the Flesh" sheets in Session 15, pgs. 104-106 for specific coping mechanisms.)

HOW IS VICTORY CONNECTED TO SPIRITUAL MATURITY?

ASK **Let the participants answer the title question before reading the paragraph.**

ASK **Describe a time you experienced victory through resting in the truth of your identity in Christ.**

ASK **Can spiritual maturity fluctuate? If so, how? If not, why not?**

A believer who is spiritually mature possesses an intimate love relationship with the Father (1 John 2:19). This bond strengthens over time by facing trials in life with faith and patient endurance (James 1:4). While God leads us into increasing spiritual maturity, the possibility exists to act immaturely through programmed flesh.

> **KEY POINT:**
> Both salvation and victory over sin come as a gift by grace through faith and not through fleshly-reliance, fleshly-effort, or fleshly-discipline.

> **KEY POINT:**
> A mature believer experiences consistent victory over sin through knowing, believing, and abiding in truth.

TRANSFORM

After meeting together, the Transform questions allow the participants to process the session's truths on their own. Review the participants' answers with them at the beginning of the next session.

PRAYER

(10 min.)

Since relationship and intimacy with God involves conversation, we encourage you to incorporate both individual and group prayer into your study.

IDENTIFYING OUR FLESH
Exposing the Counterfeit Life

15

THEME

Identifying our flesh exposes the counterfeit life so we can reject the lies and choose to walk in the Truth.

SUMMARY

Uncovering our flesh patterns may be one of the hardest exercises we will ever do. Many of us refuse to look at our own flesh because it puts us in a position of transparency and vulnerability. However, if we are not walking in the Spirit moment by moment every day, then we are walking after the flesh. We are not living out of Christ's life. Our false beliefs lead us to walk after the flesh. Until we identify our false beliefs and replace them with the truth of our identity in Christ, we will continue to walk after our flesh. This session offers step-by-step guidance for the participants to discover their false beliefs and flesh patterns.

TRANSFORM REVIEW   (10 min.)

1. How can I recognize when a thought is a lie from Satan?

The participants think about how to discern the source of thoughts. We all have many thoughts coming from different sources. Engaging in the battle means I must first pay attention to my thoughts and then discern if I am under attack. The only way to discern a lie is to know the truth.

2. When am I most susceptible to Satan's lies?

If Satan works in opportune times, recognize when those opportune times arise on an individual basis. (e.g., physical fatigue, sickness, pain, unpleasant circumstances, a certain person, etc.)

3. What lies contribute to spiritual defeat in my life?

The participants consider habitual sins or enemy strongholds in their lives. If nothing comes to mind, Session 15 is designed to expose some of those lies.

4. What thoughts or behaviors am I trying to improve through self-effort or religious performance?

This question is a lead-in to the session on identifying our flesh. For a refresher on the flesh, see Session 7.

> **TEACHING TIP:**
> Before beginning today's lesson, review the transform questions from Session 14: The Believer's Battle. The participant should have answered these alone before coming together for this session.

5. What examples of victory have I experienced in my Christian life?

This question is designed to help the participants process personal victories they have experienced in Christ. If the participants struggle to give examples, share one from your personal experience.

6. Take some time to listen. What is the Holy Spirit telling me in this session?

This question is used frequently in the Transform sections of the *Living IN Jesus* study. Continually encourage the participants to listen to the Holy Spirit for further, specific illumination. The Holy Spirit will never tell us something that contradicts Scripture.

7. How will the Holy Spirit's revelation impact my beliefs, choices, and behaviors?

Encourage the participants to express how the Holy Spirit is directing them; then support them as they follow in obedience. Real transformation occurs when beliefs correspond to changed behaviors.

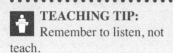 **CONNECT**   (10 min.)

 TEACHING TIP:
Remember to listen, not teach.

ASK **What has God revealed to you since we last met?**

This question opens discussion of any additional revelations not covered in the Transform review.

ASK **Why is it hard to share personal failures or struggles?**

By this point in your journey together, the participants may feel safe with you and share what they consider their own barriers to sharing personal issues with others.

ASK **How could a person benefit from reflecting on their personal history?**

This question assumes a benefit to identifying flesh. Listen for any objections or misgivings from the participants. This session requires the participants to share their deep and possibly hidden wounds or experiences. As you listen, discern their willingness to respond and be sensitive to where they are in their journey.

ASK **What makes a memory painful?**

Listen for the participants' perspectives and general conclusions of the causes of pain in events. If the participants share only the memory itself, follow-up with the question, "What made that memory painful?" Listen for unmet needs and desires.

ASK **What makes a memory good?**

Listen for the participants' perspectives of "good" and general conclusions of the causes of good in events. If the participants share only the memory itself, follow-up with the question, "What made that memory good?" Listen for met needs and desires.

RENEW   (60 min.)

EXPOSING THE COUNTERFEIT LIFE

ASK **What are flesh patterns? How do we develop them?**

Listen for the participants' perception of the flesh as taught in Session 7. Even at this point in the study, they may still be unclear regarding the flesh and its impact. The flesh is frequently confused with the sin nature and the principle of sin. Also, the enemy (the deceiver) is working to confuse this issue in a believer's understanding.

 Caution: Exposing our flesh patterns can be stressful. Reassure the participants that this exercise is an opportunity to allow God to deepen their relationship with Him. God will not condemn or punish them for what they have done or what has been done to them (Psalms 85:2; Rom 4:7; 8:1; 1 John 2:12). This exercise is a chance for them to renew their minds and experience freedom from their past. The participants may proceed with the content intellectually but resist total transparency. Be aware of any hesitancy, and pray for the right method as they approach development of their own flesh diagram.

WHY WOULD WE WANT TO LOOK AT OUR FLESH PATTERNS?

ASK **Have you discovered any of your false beliefs? If so, how?**

Review the participants' answers from question #3 in the Transform section of Session 7. Be ready to share your personal discoveries if they have not answered the question.

SPECIFIC REASONS TO LOOK AT OUR FLESH PATTERNS

After reading the five specific reasons listed in the Participant's Guide, ask the participants to answer the following questions:

ASK **Which one of these reasons concerns you the most?**

ASK **Which one of these reasons excites you the most?**

 Teaching Tip: As the Spirit leads, continue to use your own journey as an example where applicable. Believers who have embraced their freedom in Christ are willing to be transparent. The purpose of self-disclosure is not to draw attention to self, but rather is a means of ministering to others who are hurting (2 Cor. 1:3-4).

KEY POINT:
This session's purpose is to ask God to expose our flesh so we can walk more consistently in the victory found in submitting to the Holy Spirit.

KEY POINT:
Until we face our false beliefs and replace them with the truth, we will continue to walk after our flesh.

KEY POINT:
We look at our flesh patterns to expose false identities, to expose alternate need-meeters, to enjoy healthier relationships, to heal from past hurts through forgiveness, and to learn how our emotions correlate with our beliefs.

• • • • • • • • • • • • • • • • • • • •
KEY POINT:
We must know and believe our new identity in Christ before we begin to discover our flesh patterns. Otherwise, we will find it difficult to objectively analyze our behavior and the underlying false beliefs.

FIRST STEP: STAND CONFIDENTLY IN OUR NEW IDENTITY

ASK What is your identity?

ASK Which aspects of your position as a child of God do you really enjoy? (Refer to Session 10.)

This question reviews and brings the participants to the point of identifying the flesh. If the participants know their identity well, it is not necessary to review Session 10.

SECOND STEP: FILLING IN OUR OWN FLESH DIAGRAMS

Teaching Tip: Before taking the participants through a few events, it may prove helpful to share with the participants completed worksheets on your own flesh patterns. It is vital that you recognize your own fleshly coping mechanisms. If you have been reluctant to examine part(s) of your own story and belief system, ask the Holy Spirit to reveal the reason; only then can you journey with someone else to understand their flesh.

HELPING PARTICIPANTS COMPLETE THEIR FLESH WORKSHEETS

A. General Guidelines

1. **In order for this session to be effective, people must have a safe place** to talk openly and honestly about themselves. To create a safe place:

   • Accept one another (Rom. 15:7).

   • Suspend judgment (Rom. 14:12-14).

   • Maintain confidentiality (2 Tim. 2:16-17).

   • Give grace (Eph. 4:29).

   • Refrain from "fixing" and "rescuing" each other and allow the Holy Spirit to do the work (Phil. 2:12-13).

   In order to create a safe place, the equipper must be a safe person. As a leader, you can exhibit these qualities and encourage others in making a group safe to learn and grow openly and honestly. If you do not have a safe group, consider walking through this session one-on-one with members of your group.

2. **Remember the goal** is for you to experience Christ's life. You cannot control whether or not the people you are equipping "see" their flesh and/or live in freedom (be careful not to make it "all about you").

3. **Remember the Counselor (John 14:26).** The Holy Spirit is the Wonderful Counselor. We cannot open a person's eyes to the bankruptcy of the flesh, his/her belief system, and his/her coping mechanisms by our history-taking efforts. Only the Holy Spirit can do this job.

4. **As often as the Holy Spirit prompts you, remind the participants that their behavior does not equal their identity.**

5. **Listen, listen, listen.** You do not have to fill every box immediately.

6. **Do not assume** you know how they feel or what they believe simply because you have had a similar experience or you know someone who has. Always ask questions to clarify.

7. **Use language that matches the content, meaning, and intensity of what they have shared** (without repeating word for word). If they say they were enraged, do not say, "It sounds like you were frustrated." Rather, you could say, "It sounds like you were very angry."

8. **The issue is not the circumstance (event), but their belief (message) and reaction (behavior).** You do not need to discuss other people or events in detail except in terms of how it affected them. When they share about someone else in their lives or some event that occurred to someone else, turn the conversation around to focus on them and how it affected their belief systems. Divert the discussion from excusing others' behavior or blaming them. Remember, we are only pursuing events in order to discover lies believed and resulting flesh patterns.

9. **How in-depth must you go to reveal a person's history?** The Holy Spirit will guide you to pursue enough history to reveal the participants' own feelings, beliefs, and fleshly coping patterns; spouses, kids, circumstances, etc., are not the problem.

10. **As the equipper walking with someone sharing their history, be willing to risk making a mistake in listening, understanding, or asking questions.** The success of this process does not depend on your perfection, but on God's revelation. A resistance to surrender the right to be perfect can inadvertently cause the equipper to operate from his or her flesh. This can result in focusing on your own performance rather than empathizing with the participants.

11. **Use the included sheets** (Typical Beliefs pp 100-101, Feeling Words pp 102-103, and Manifestation of the Flesh pp 104-106) to help participants identify beliefs, feelings, and behaviors.

B. Where to Begin

The order of content in an event column is laid out sequentially, indicated by an arrow. The enemy uses an event (opportune time) to introduce a false message or belief. When this lie is believed, negative feelings and behaviors result. However, when diagramming the flesh, you do not have to start at the top and go down the column.

C. Conversational Entry Points to Help Fill Each Event Column

The participant may make statements that do not correspond to the listed order of the worksheet. Follow their thought process, and ask clarifying questions to identify the needed information. For example:

1. **Age** – "Middle school was a brutal time for me."

   - Write "middle school" in the "Age" box.
   - A possible question to ask in order to fill out the rest of the column is, "What made middle school so brutal?" (Event)

2. **Person** – "I was much closer to mom than I was to dad."

   - You can begin with either "mom" or "dad".
   - Write "mom" in the "Person" box.

- A question to help fill out the rest of the column might be, "What made you closer to mom?" (Event)

- Begin another event column starting with "dad".

- Write "dad" in the "Person" box.

- A question to help fill out the rest of the column might be, "What did your dad do that made you closer to mom?" (Event)

3. **Message** – "I was the runt of the family."

   - Write "I was the runt of the family" in the "Message/Beliefs" box.

   - A clarifying question to help fill out the rest of the column might be, "What does it say about you that you are the runt of the family?" (Messages/Beliefs).

   - Other questions to help fill out the rest of the column might include, "What made you believe you were the runt in the family?" (Event) or, "How do you feel about being the runt of the family?" (Feelings)

4. **Feelings** – "I am so stressed."

   - Write "stressed" in the "Feelings" box,

   - A question to help fill out the rest of the column might be, "What happened that has led to your stress?" (Event)

   - Feelings are usually indicators of beliefs. If the participants have difficulty identifying the messages or beliefs, explore their feelings to guide them into awareness of their beliefs.

5. **Behaviors** – "I am a control freak."

   - In order to clarify their behavior, a possible question to ask is, "What are you doing that makes you think you are a control freak?" Write their answers in the "Behaviors" box.

   - A question to help fill out the rest of the column might be, "What are you feeling when you attempt to control?" (Feelings)

   - Other questions you might ask are, "At the moment you are controlling, what are you believing about yourself?", "What are you trying to accomplish?", or, "What kind of person is a control freak?" (Messages/ Beliefs)

D. Useful Approaches to Help Participants Identify the Message/Belief

1. **Rephrase the question** from "What did that say about you?" to "What need was not met when that event happened?"

2. **Shift the point of reference** (examples: "If you said or did that to your son/daughter, how would they feel? What would it say to them?"; "If I went through something similar, what might it have said to me?")

3. **Use the "Remote Control of Life."** Rewind them to the moment of the event and pause the event; then ask them to view it as a child. For example, a participant was bullied in the schoolyard. Ask the participant to describe the scene, words, and actions. Then tell the participant to pause in the moment and ask "What were you feeling in that moment?" "What did that say about you?"

4. **Remind the participants** the focus of this exercise is on the message they received. The participants may say the message from the event is only about the other person. Redirect using one of the approaches listed above.

5. **Wait on the Holy Spirit.** It is ok to leave a box blank or put a question mark there. Encourage them to ask the Spirit about it at a later time.

EXAMPLE FLESH DIAGRAM – PERSON 1

	EVENT 3	EVENT 4	EVENT 5	
	10+ yrs. old	15 yrs. old	High School	AGE
	Sisters	Girl	Peers	PERSON
	Picked on me, teased me	Took her to dance. She danced with older boys and never with me.	Achieved – sports, humor, party-guy	EVENT
	• I am weak, or helpless. • I don't have what it takes.	• I am unlikeable. • I am not strong enough to stand up for myself.	• I am loved and accepted. • I am admired and respected (as long as I do well).	MESSAGES/ BELIEFS
	Helpless Powerless!! Anxious	Helpless Hurt Ashamed	Good Happy	FEELINGS
	• Laughed it off, acted like it didn't bother me • Stuffed my emotions • Avoided conflict	Excelled in sports, dominate in that arena	• Kept doing it, • Achieved more in sports, • Tried to be a bigger partier & drinker	BEHAVIORS
	I am powerful 2 Tim. 1:7	I am dearly loved. 1 John 3:1	I am loved unconditionally. Rom. 8:38-39	TRUTH

EXAMPLE FLESH DIAGRAM - PERSON 2

	EVENT 6	EVENT 7	EVENT 8
AGE	Adult (mom)	Adult (wife)	Adult
PERSON	Daughter	Husband	Myself
EVENT	Daughter is making poor choices in life-style and habits	Husband is verbally abusing me.	I am depressed and don't know why.
MESSAGES/ BELIEFS	• I am a complete failure as a mom. • I am not respected. • I am not valuable.	• I am weak. • I am not safe. • I am out of control.	• I am a depressed person. • There is something wrong with me. • I am defective. • I am alone.
FEELINGS	Devastated Depressed Embarrassed Helpless	Terrified Anxious Humiliated Powerless	Sad, Depressed Miserable, Hopeless
BEHAVIORS	Try to fix daughter, Remove her temptations, Spy on her, Threatened her, yelled at her	Cower, Blame myself (I deserve this), Cry & go into a shell, Walk on eggshells	• Isolate and avoid others • Stay in bed a lot • Medicate • Blame myself
TRUTH	I am adequate 2 Cor. 3:5 I am loved & God will work this for my good Rom. 8:28, 37-39	I am valuable Luke 12:24 I am rescued. Col. 1:13	I am complete Col. 2:10 I am loved 1 John 3:1-3

TRANSFORM

After meeting together, the Transform questions allow the participants to process the session's truths on their own. Review the participants' answers with them at the beginning of the next session.

PRAYER   (10 min.)

Since relationship and intimacy with God involves conversation, we encourage you to incorporate both individual and group prayer into your study.

BROKENNESS AND SURRENDER
Unveiling Life

16

THEME

Suffering that leads to brokenness and surrender, will unveil God's life in and through us.

SUMMARY

God uses burdens in our lives to bring about brokenness. In the midst of suffering He often reveals counterfeit need-meeters and our futile strategies of dependence on our own resources. God leads us to surrender our rights, allowing us to experience His abundant supply. As we surrender rights, we experience the love, joy, and peace found in Christ's life.

TRANSFORM REVIEW   (10 min.)

1. As I record different events on my diagram, what feelings regularly surface?

The participants have the opportunity to become aware of dominant, recurring feelings. The diagram reveals any current battles triggered by the same emotions.

2. As I record different events on my diagram, what false beliefs repeat?

The participants should recognize dominant, recurring beliefs. Now they can take the thoughts captive, recognize the lies, and replace them with the truth of the participants' identity in Christ (Session 14).

3. How do my flesh patterns impact my relationships with others today?

The participants consider the impact of dominant, recurring behaviors. Now they can recognize when a fleshly behavior has impacted a relationship. The participants may be led by the Spirit to ask forgiveness (Session 17).

4. How will understanding my flesh patterns help me embrace the truth?

The participants move past the discovery of lies and away from the habits (flesh patterns), toward believing and trusting in the truth. As God reveals the bankruptcy (or futility) of our fleshly behavior, we place more value on the truth.

> **TEACHING TIP:**
> Before beginning today's lesson, review the transform questions from Session 15: Identifying Our Flesh. The participant should have answered these alone before coming together for this session.

CONNECT   (10 min.)

TEACHING TIP:
Remember to listen, not teach.

ASK What has God revealed to you since we last met?

Discuss any additional revelations not covered in the Transform review.

ASK Why does God allow suffering and pain in your life?

The participants should express their understanding of the purpose of suffering and also God's role. Listen for the participants' understanding or opinion of the suffering and pain.

ASK How do you handle suffering and pain in your life?

The participants can honestly express how they have handled or are handling suffering, which may or may not have been in a biblical way. Responses indicate their understanding of how God desires us to walk through the suffering and pain we all face in this world.

ASK Think of an instance of significant personal suffering. What do you believe God was doing in that time?

The participants have a chance to explain what God was doing in their personal experience. The participants may express hostility towards God during this time. When difficult, painful, or evil things happen to us, we can be tempted to doubt God, think evil of Him, or even doubt His existence. During this connect time, do not be defensive and argue with the participants about the existence or goodness of God. Instead, their responses provide insight into their spiritual maturity and any renewing still needed in their mind. As you go through the renew section together, ask the Holy Spirit to minister His love and truth to them.

RENEW   (60 min.)

KEY POINT:
A burden is something difficult or hard that is out of our control. A temptation is a mental attack from Satan, who uses the world and our flesh to distract us from believing God's truths and living out of His life.

BURDENS, TEMPTATIONS, AND OUR ABILITIES

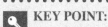

ASK What burdens have you experienced?

It may be helpful for you to disclose one or two of your burdens (past or current). Be brief in sharing so that the participants have ample time to share.

ILLUSTRATION: DIFFERENCE BETWEEN TEMPTATIONS AND BURDENS.

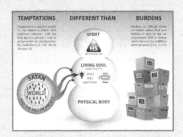

ASK **Will God allow us to experience a burden greater than we can handle?**

The answer is yes. An example is found in 2 Corinthians 1:8-9 (in the margin). Because people often confuse burdens and temptations, they mistakenly attribute the promise relating to temptations found in 1 Corinthians 10:13 and apply it to burdens. God does not allow us to experience a temptation beyond what we can bear, but He does allow us to experience burdens too heavy for us to carry.

BURDENS BRING SUFFERING

ASK **Which of these types of suffering have you experienced? – Spiritual? Mental? Emotional? or Physical?**

You may refer to an experience the participants shared in Session 15. Also, you may share one or two of your own experiences, but be brief and allow the participants more time to speak.

PURPOSE OF BURDENS AND SUFFERING

ASK **In what ways does dependency on God lead to greater intimacy?**

Possible answers: trust that grows as He faithfully provides, increased awareness of God's character (especially His intimate love, care, and compassion) and His ability to meet our needs, etc.

SUFFERING THAT LEADS TO BROKENNESS

ASK **What are the possible responses to suffering?**

Let the participants answer first. Two responses to suffering are resistance and surrender. Acts 7:51 shows an example of those who resist while 2 Corinthians 12:9 displays an example of surrender.

ASK **Describe a time when you have blamed God or have been tempted to blame Him.**

If the participants have never blamed God nor have been tempted to blame Him, you might ask if they know someone who has blamed God.

ASK **How has God used suffering to reveal your flesh patterns?**

If the participants have difficulty answering, share your own experiences of how suffering revealed your flesh patterns.

KEY POINT: Suffering is the pain we experience from the loss of something we value.

KEY POINT: God uses burdens in our lives to take us beyond our own resources so we will grow in dependence on Him.

KEY POINT: When we respond to suffering with brokenness and surrender, we more fully display the life of God which dwells in us.

• • • • • • • • • • • • • • • • • •

KEY POINT:
God leads us to surrender all of our rights to Him, acknowledging that He is our life and is sufficient to meet all of our needs.

SURRENDERING RIGHTS

 **What is a right?**

Ask this question before you begin this sub-section.

 **What rights do you hold tightly? What needs are you trying to meet by holding onto those rights?**

The participants discover their own rights and make the connection between needs and rights.

 TRANSFORM

After meeting together, the Transform questions allow the participants to process the session's truths on their own. Review the participants' answers with them at the beginning of the next session.

PRAYER   (10 min.)

The closing prayer in this session is the prayer of surrender. Ask the participants to list the rights they are surrendering in the blanks provided. Ask them to sign and date the provided spaces below the prayer. Their signature and date are simply reminders of their intentional decision to surrender their stated rights to God. Satan will tempt the participants to hold onto those rights in the future. This signed prayer reminds the participant of the decision they made. The participants can re-state this decision as the enemy attempts to deceive them to reclaim these rights. For example, someone may treat the participants disrespectfully in the future. The temptation will be to reclaim the right to be respected and to respond to the other person with disrespect or unkindness. The participants can take that thought captive and determine to continue to surrender the right to be respected to God.

17

GIVING AND ASKING FORGIVENESS
Releasing Life

THEME

Giving and asking forgiveness removes the cause of bitterness and releases Christ's life to flow freely through a believer.

SUMMARY

If we walk after the flesh, we will hurt and offend each other. God's full forgiveness and our new nature in Christ enable us to forgive. We can choose to forgive the offender by releasing the debt owed and letting go of the hurt and anger. When we offend another, we can seek forgiveness by taking responsibility for our action and asking for forgiveness. We can choose to surrender to the Holy Spirit and express Christ's life through forgiveness, whether a relationship is reconciled or not.

TRANSFORM REVIEW   (10 min.)

1. What burdens and suffering have I experienced?

Listen for any new burdens the participants did not disclose in the previous session.

2. In what ways have my burdens and suffering led me to greater dependence on God?

The participants should connect their suffering to greater dependence on God. Ask them for specific lessons they have learned and decisions they have made.

3. In what ways have I continued to rely on the flesh despite my burdens and suffering?

The participants should acknowledge areas of resistance (strongholds) and bring those (rights not yet surrendered) to God. This question connects with the next question (#4) to complete the evaluation.

4. What keeps me from surrendering my rights?

The participants further explore any circumstances, lies, or emotions which can influence them more than God's opinion. Examples are: a false concept of God, pride, the deception that people or possessions meet my needs, excessive focus on painful emotions, a desperation for relief instead of a desire to identify God's purpose, etc.

5. What specific rights (perceived entitlements) have I not surrendered to God?

> **TEACHING TIP:**
> Before beginning today's lesson, review the transform questions from Session 16: Brokenness and Surrender. The participant should have answered these alone before coming together for this session.

The participants select any rights they have not surrendered from the list provided. The rights listed are possible responses, but the list is not exhaustive. Encourage the participant to add in the blanks provided additional rights the Holy Spirit reveals. The rights the participants select can now be used in the prayer of surrender for that session.

 ## CONNECT   (10 min.)

 TEACHING TIP:
Remember to listen, not teach.

ASK **What has God revealed to you since we last met?**

This question opens discussion of any additional revelations not covered in the Transform review.

ASK **How do you respond when someone hurts or offends you?**

Possible answers: withdrawing, defensiveness, violence, sarcasm, crying, etc. It might be helpful to refer to the participants' flesh events recorded in their history worksheets (Session 15).

ASK **What happens to a relationship when there is a hurt or offense?**

A good follow-up might be to ask for an example from their relationships with family or friends.

ASK **In what ways do people reconcile with each other?**

The participants' share their understanding or experiences with two individuals attempting to reconcile a damaged relationship. Possible answers: act like it is not important, stop thinking about it, tell yourself it did not hurt, etc.

 ## RENEW   (60 min.)

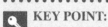 **KEY POINT:**
A person who experiences hurt from rejection often feels anger, which can lead to bitterness and fleshly behaviors to cope with the pain.

GIVING FORGIVENESS

ASK **Let the participants answer the question "What happens to us when we experience rejection?" before reading the paragraph.**

Since a similar question was asked in "Connect," refer to that discussion and ask the participants to expand their answer if necessary.

ASK **Why do we sometimes embrace anger?**

People may choose anger as the pathway to resolving hurt. Possible answers:

- It is a powerful motivator to pay back another person.

- It gives us a sense of power. Extended anger makes us feel safe by insulating us from the hurt.

- If we do not maintain our anger, the offender will not suffer any consequences, etc.

WHAT DOES GOD WANT US TO DO IF WE EXPERIENCE HURT AND ANGER?

`ASK`   Let the participants answer the title question before the sub-section.

`ASK`   What might keep you from releasing your hurt and anger to God?

Possible answers: false concept of God, false beliefs listed in the illustrations, expectations, etc.

ILLUSTRATION: BELIEFS THAT KEEP US HOLDING ON TO OUR HURTS.

If we hold onto offenses, they become dead weight and prevent us from moving with the Spirit to experience God's love, joy, and peace.

`ASK`   Which one of the four belief statements have you believed in the past?

The participants expose the debt or conditions they may have placed on their offender(s). Depending on their answers, good follow-up questions might be: "What conditions are you placing on the offender to manage your hurt?", "How does the offender's suffering, exposure, or change remove your hurt?" (Only Christ can remove the hurt, but this question helps the participants realize where they may be tempted to look to deal with their past.)

WHAT ENABLES US TO FORGIVE?

`ASK`   Let the participants answer the title question before reading the paragraph.

`ASK`   What do you think about the statement, "It is our nature (most natural inclination) to forgive"?

The aspect of being a forgiver as an identity statement may be difficult for the participants to embrace. Follow-up questions might be: "How does love relate to forgiveness?", "Do you contain the fullness of God's love?", "Are you, by nature, able to love others unconditionally?"

HOW DO WE FORGIVE ANOTHER?

`ASK`   Let the participants answer the title question before reading the paragraph.

`ASK`   Why is acknowledging the hurt important?

Without acknowledging the hurt there is nothing to forgive.

`ASK`   Why is it important to acknowledge your feelings?

KEY POINT:
As we release the debt, we let go of the hurt and anger. This allows the expression of Christ's life to flow through us.

KEY POINT:
Our ability to forgive is based on two truths: 1) we are completely forgiven by God, and 2) it is our nature to forgive as new creations.

KEY POINT:
The indwelling Spirit empowers and guides us to forgive others immediately and continuously.

Acknowledging your emotions can bring hurtful messages into the light and allow you to fully release the debt.

ASK **Does accepting the person unconditionally mean condoning their behavior? Why or why not?**

God has accepted us unconditionally and yet does not condone our sinful behavior. Love is a choice to act in another's best interest regardless of their behavior. You can address inappropriate behavior in a way that expresses love.

ASK **What does it look like to go forward in a relationship as if the offense had not occurred?**

True forgiveness means never bringing up the offense again (Love keeps no record of wrongs). Also, you do not allow the previous offense to affect how you see or accept (love and value) the other person.

ASK **Which of these steps is most difficult for you? Why?**

WHAT ARE SOME MISCONCEPTIONS ABOUT FORGIVING?

ASK **Let the participants answer the title question before reading the paragraph.**

ASK **Which of these statements have deceived you and kept you from choosing forgiveness?**

1. Forgiveness requires that I no longer feel angry.

ASK **Why is this statement a deception?**

Forgiveness is not based on emotions, but it is a choice to release the debt to God. Possible follow-up questions: "What is the danger of waiting for the correct emotions to forgive?", "When can you confidently say you will never be angry about the offense?"

2. The passage of time or the process of forgetting leads to forgiveness.

ASK **Why is this statement a deception?**

Forgiveness is not based on the passage of time. Possible follow-up questions: "At what point in this statement has the person made a conscious decision to release the debt?", "Why do people think the passage of time will lead to forgiveness?"

The process of forgetting does not lead to forgiveness because it still does not acknowledge the offense. Forgiveness is acknowledging the offense and choosing to give it to God.

3. Saying, "Let's just forget about it" or denying I have really been hurt; believing forgiveness is pretending the hurt was really not that bad.

KEY POINT:
Holding on to misconceptions about forgiveness will keep us from forgiving others.

`ASK` **Why is this statement a deception?**

Forgiveness is acknowledging the offense and choosing to give it to God. People pleasing, conflict avoidance, and fear of appearing weak lead to pretending the offense did not hurt. When people suppress or deny hurt, they respond in anger indirectly (sarcasm, passive-aggressive behavior, gossip, internalization resulting in physical/mental health issues, etc.).

4. Forgiveness is justifying, understanding, or explaining away someone's rejecting behavior.

`ASK` **Why is this statement a deception?**

Forgiving is not the same as saying the offense was acceptable. Attempts to explain or excuse the offense or the offender may improve your feelings. However, it still does not acknowledge the offense, allowing you to release the debt. The ability to forgive does not come from a clear understanding of the reason for the offense.

5. Forgiveness means I must tell the offender/s I forgive them.

`ASK` **Why is this statement a deception?**

Telling the other person "I forgive you" is not a condition for forgiveness nor is it necessary once you forgive.

ASKING FORGIVENESS

`ASK` **Why do you think God desires reconciliation?**

God is love and values relationships (Session 1). Reconciliation is simply restoring people to healthy, loving relationships.

HINDRANCES TO ASKING FORGIVENESS

`ASK` **What keeps people from asking forgiveness?**

Ask this question before covering the list of hindrances. This question allows the participants to answer in reference to people in general.

`ASK` **Which of the items listed in the workbook have hindered you from asking forgiveness?**

Ask this question after covering the list of hindrances. This review will lead to personal reflection.

HOW DO WE ASK FORGIVENESS?

`ASK` **Let the participants answer the title question before reading the paragraph.**

KEY POINT:
God's heart is for reconciliation. He desires for us to initiate reconciliation with anyone we have offended.

KEY POINT:
Satan will send lies to hinder us from asking forgiveness.

KEY POINT:
As the Holy Spirit leads, our path to asking forgiveness will be unique to our journey but will include certain important elements.

ASK **Which of these steps are important? Why?**

If the participants do not think certain steps are important, read the corresponding Scriptures and discuss.

ASK **Which of these steps are difficult for you? Why?**

If the participants are experiencing difficulty with one or more of these steps, ask, "What do you think is the underlying reason causing the difficulty?" Refer to "Hindrances To Asking Forgiveness" if there is a problem identifying underlying reasons.

WHAT IF THEY DO NOT FORGIVE US?

ASK **Let the participants answer the title question before reading the paragraph.**

ASK **Have you ever had your request for forgiveness rejected? If so, how did you respond?**

Possible follow-up question: Was your response healthy? Why or why not?

If the participants have not had a forgiveness request rejected, ask the next question.

ASK **How would you feel if someone did not forgive you? What would you do with those feelings?**

If the participants have an unhealthy reaction, guide them through the concepts of their flesh patterns, surrendering rights (the right to be forgiven and have a healthy relationship), and giving forgiveness (when the other person has rejected you).

DOES FORGIVENESS ALWAYS LEAD TO RECONCILIATION?

ASK **Let the participants answer the title question before reading the paragraph.**

ASK **What does reconciliation in a relationship that has been damaged look like to you?**

Reconciliation is restored harmony and intimacy. The process of reconciliation varies according to the offense and the individuals.

ASK **Which, if any, of your past or current relationships remain unreconciled?**

Possible follow-up questions: Have you tried to reconcile? If so, what happened? If not, why not?

· · · · · · · · · · · · · · · · · · ·

KEY POINT:
If our request for forgiveness is not accepted, we pray for the other person and rest in God to heal the relationship.

· · · · · · · · · · · · · · · · · · ·

KEY POINT:
Reconciliation is only possible when both people are willing.

ASK **How do you experience Christ's life when you are rejected by someone with whom you wish to be reconciled?**

Possible truths to review: identity, intimacy with God, bringing burdens to God, fruit of the Spirit, believer's battle.

TRANSFORM

After meeting together, the Transform questions allow the participants to process the session's truths on their own. Review the participants' answers with them at the beginning of the next session.

PRAYER   (10 min.)

Since relationship and intimacy with God involves conversation, we encourage you to incorporate both individual and group prayer into your study.

18

LAW VS. GRACE
Bondage vs. Life

THEME

Living by law leads to bondage, whereas living by God's grace is living out of His life.

SUMMARY

Our relationship with God is no longer achieved by performance in a law system. We who are in Christ now enjoy a relationship characterized by God's grace. This New Covenant is determined by who He is and what He has already accomplished (performed for us) and then gifted to us in Christ.

TRANSFORM REVIEW   (10 min.)

1. Forgiving People who have hurt me in the Past: The Empty Chair Exercise

If the participants do not want to share any of their experiences of forgiving, share one of your own. Resist the urge to force them to share. Depend on the Holy Spirit to do His work.

2. Asking Forgiveness of People I Have Hurt in the Past

If the participants do not want to share any of their experiences of asking forgiveness, share one of your own. Resist the urge to force them to share. Depend on the Holy Spirit to do His work.

> **TEACHING TIP:**
> Before beginning today's lesson, review the transform questions from Session 17: Giving and Asking Forgiveness. The participant should have worked through the forgiveness worksheets alone before coming together for this session.

CONNECT   (10 min.)

ASK **What has God revealed to you since we last met?**

Discuss any additional revelations not covered in the "Transform" review.

ASK **What was the purpose of God's Law?**

This question is designed to help you discover how the participants perceive the purpose of law in their lives. A good clarifying question may be, "What are some of God's Laws?"

> **TEACHING TIP:**
> Remember to listen, not teach.

ASK **What does it mean to live under laws?**

This question encourages the participants to think about what life is like under laws. A good follow-up question may be "What laws do you live under?"

ASK **What is the role of God's grace?**

Listen for the participants' understanding of the role of God's grace. A follow-up question might be "What is grace?"

ASK **How did Jesus demonstrate God's grace?**

The participants' responses will give you a clue to how well they understand the concept of God's grace. Jesus demonstrated God's grace in a myriad of ways (John 1:14). In case the participants cannot think of any examples, here are a few:

- Jesus turned water into wine to save the groom the embarrassment of running out of wine at his wedding.

- Jesus offered living water to the Samaritan woman at the well.

- Jesus gave undeserved favor to the woman caught in adultery.

- Jesus healed the severed ear of the soldier who came to arrest Him.

- Jesus forgave and accepted the criminal on the cross next to Him.

RENEW   (60 min.)

KEY POINT:
Law is a system of demands placed on behavior with blessings for those who obey and curses for those who disobey.

WHAT IS LAW?

ASK **Let the participants answer the title question before reading the following paragraph.**

ASK **What are some of God's laws given to the Israelites?**

The participants explore the meaning of law by naming a few.

ASK **What were some blessings Israel experienced by keeping God's law?**

Refer to Deuteronomy 11 and 28 for examples.

ASK **What were some curses Israel experienced by breaking God's law?**

Refer to Deuteronomy 11 and 28 for examples.

ASK **What benefits do we enjoy because of laws in our society?**

Possible answers: safer driving (traffic laws), ability to secure the rights to property (property laws), protection from injustice (civil laws), freedom of speech (Bill of Rights), etc.

WHAT ARE LIMITATIONS OF GOD'S LAW?

ASK Let the participants answer the title question before reading the following paragraph.

ASK Describe the limitations you face when you attempt to improve, or correct, wrong behavior by following God's Laws. Give some specific examples.

Possible answers: no power, motivation from fear and insecurity instead of love and acceptance, pride, judgmentalism, etc.

ASK What does oxygen do to fire? Similarly, in what ways does the law stimulate your flesh?

Oxygen causes fire to rapidly grow. In the same way, the Law arouses sinful flesh. (e.g., If a sign says, "Wet Paint - Do Not Touch," it may tempt you to touch the object to see if the paint is wet.)

WHAT DOES LIVING BY A LAW SYSTEM PRODUCE?

ASK Let the participants answer the title question before reading the following paragraph.

ASK When you are successful in keeping the rules, how does it feel? How does that impact your thoughts about yourself?

If you discern an attitude of pride, use these possible follow-up questions: How did this affect your behavior? How did this affect your attitude towards others? Where are you placing your confidence? What are you trying to achieve?

ASK When you fail at keeping God's laws, how do you handle your failure?

Possible answers: give up, try harder, medicate or escape, pretend like you are doing ok (wear a mask), confess, beat yourself up, etc.

WHAT RESOURCES ARE EMPLOYED WHEN WE LIVE BY A LAW SYSTEM?

ASK Let the participants answer the title question before reading the paragraph.

ASK How have you attempted to formulate your own rules or laws to manage a personal struggle? Did it work?

Some examples: a diet program for weight management, counting to 10 before speaking when you are angry, read self-help books, write a letter to an offender and then rip it up, etc.

KEY POINT:
The Law shows us the right way to live but does not make us acceptable or provide the power to obey.

KEY POINT:
Living by a law system can produce unhealthy pride, shame, guilt, and condemnation, which lead to a judgmental attitude and/or using a mask to hide failures.

KEY POINT:
Under a law system, a person utilizes physical resources (flesh) to keep moral standards and attain a fulfilled life.

🔑 **KEY POINT:**
Jesus' sinless life and death fulfilled the Law and restored humanity to a receiving system under a new covenant of grace.

🔑 **KEY POINT:**
The grace system is an unconditional receiving system where we are blessed based on Christ's finished work.

🔑 **KEY POINT:**
Through the work of Christ's death, burial, and resurrection, God took us out of Adam and placed us into Christ, changing our covenant relationship from a Law system to a grace system.

🔑 **KEY POINT:**
The grace of God gives us the desire to do what is right and the freedom and power to live it out.

ASK **Describe a time when you tried to keep one of God's commandments. Was your focus on God's provision or your self-effort?**

If the participants cannot think of a time, share one from your experience.

TIME FOR A NEW SYSTEM

ASK **Why is it impossible for a person to attain righteousness by keeping the Law?**

Everyone is born dead in Adam. Dead people only have flesh as a resource; therefore, no one is able to keep the Law. (Review problem #2 from Session 8 if necessary.)

WHAT IS A GRACE SYSTEM?

ASK **Let the participants answer the title question before before reading the following paragraph.**

ASK **Have you ever been gifted something for no reason? If yes, how did that make you feel toward the giver? Toward yourself?**

If the participants are operating from a grace system, they may express an attitude of thankfulness and gratitude toward the giver. If they are operating from a law system, they may express feelings of obligation toward the giver ("I need to pay you back.") or unworthiness toward themselves ("I don't deserve this.").

HOW DID GOD TRANSFER US FROM A LAW SYSTEM TO A GRACE SYSTEM?

ASK **Let the participants answer the title question before reading the following paragraph.**

If anything about this transfer from Law to grace is confusing, review Sessions 8 and 9.

ILLUSTRATION: MARRIED TO MR. LAW OR MR. GRACE (ROM. 7:1-6)?

Review the guide to this illustration on page 167 of the *Living IN Jesus* Participant's Guide. This illustration is a visual illustration of Romans 7:1-6.

WHAT DOES IT MEAN TO LIVE BY GRACE?

ASK **Let the participants answer the title question before reading the following paragraph.**

ASK What do you want your Christian life to look like? How do you accomplish that?

These questions will gauge the participants' understanding of living by grace versus living under law. If they are still struggling with a law system mentality, their answer will include religious works they must do. If they are understanding grace, their answer will focus more on their relationship with God.

ASK Which is the better motivation – fear of condemnation because of failure to keep the law or the love and grace of God? Explain.

Listen to determine if the participants understand why the motivation of fear under a law system is inadequate to change behavior.

ASK As a believer, do you have a desire to sin or to not sin?

Are the participants owning the truth of their new identity in Christ by understanding that they do not have a desire to sin? If not, review Session 9 and 10.

ASK How does living under a grace system change your view of God? yourself? others?

This question allows the participants to make practical connections between the concept of grace and how grace is manifested through their thoughts, attitudes, and actions. Some examples: going from achieving to receiving, moving from demanding to gratitude, going from frustration to patience, etc.

ILLUSTRATION: TWO SYSTEMS OF LIVING

Review the guide to this illustration on page 168 of the *Living IN Jesus* Participant's Guide. This illustration shows the difference between behavior generated from God's life within and behavior produced from self-effort in an attempt to be good and do what is right.

TRANSFORM

After meeting together, the Transform questions allow the participants to process the session's truths on their own. Review the participants' answers with them at the beginning of the next session.

PRAYER   (10 min.)

Since relationship and intimacy with God involves conversation, we encourage you to incorporate both individual and group prayer into your study.

19

RELATING UNCONDITIONALLY
Sharing Life

THEME

Believers can share life with others by God's grace instead of placing others under law.

SUMMARY

Relationships based on expectations (laws) are unhealthy and produce anger, hurt, frustration, and sorrow. Relationships based on grace release others from the performance expectations of living under law. Giving grace to others fosters healthy relationships by providing an atmosphere where intimacy can flourish and people can grow in Christ.

TRANSFORM REVIEW   (10 min.)

1. What laws have I tried to keep?

The participants focus on rules or laws which govern their lives. Possible categories: Christian growth (Bible study, prayer), civic (traffic, stealing, taxes) or personal conduct (dieting, managing an addiction).

2. What masks do I use to hide my failure to perform?

Possible answers: smiling, being friendly, sarcasm, humor, lying, exaggerating, religious activity, avoiding situations that can produce failure, etc.

3. What beliefs lead me to operate under a law system even though I have been set free?

The participants explore their belief system about God and about their own selves. Possible answers: I am not accepted unless I perform well. God only blesses people who perform well. God is a harsh taskmaster. Etc.

4. In what ways can I transition from a law system to a grace system?

This question leads the participants to consider action steps to transition. Their answers should include: acknowledging false beliefs, taking thoughts captive, believing truth, and responding with action.

5. Take some time to listen. What is the Holy Spirit telling me in this session?

This question is used frequently in the Transform sections of the *Living IN Jesus* study. Continually encourage the participants to listen to the Holy Spirit for further, specific illumination. The Holy Spirit will never tell us something that contradicts Scripture.

 TEACHING TIP: Before beginning today's lesson, review the transform questions from Session 18: Law vs. Grace. The participant should have answered these alone before coming together for this session.

6. How will the Holy Spirit's revelation impact my beliefs, choices, and behaviors?

Encourage the participants to express how the Holy Spirit is directing them; then support them as they follow in obedience. Real transformation occurs when beliefs correspond to changed behaviors.

 CONNECT   (10 min.)

 TEACHING TIP:
Remember to listen, not teach.

ASK **What has God revealed to you since we last met?**

This question opens discussion of any additional revelations not covered in the Transform review.

ASK **What conditions or expectations do people place on others?**

Explore the participants' perception of conditional acceptance. Possible answers: being faithful, listening without interrupting, being punctual, returning phone calls, religious expectations, etc.

ASK **How are relationships affected by conditions or expectations?**

Explore the participants' awareness of relational consequences. Possible answers: damages intimacy; leads to hostility or avoidance; breaks trust; leads to frustration, rejection, hopelessness, etc.

ASK **What does a grace filled relationship look like?**

Listen for the participants' concept of grace as it is shared in relationships. Possible answers: forgiveness, acceptance, generosity toward each other, etc.

 RENEW   (60 min.)

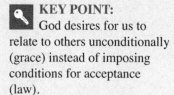 **KEY POINT:**
God desires for us to relate to others unconditionally (grace) instead of imposing conditions for acceptance (law).

KEY POINT:
A law-based relationship focuses on living up to each other's expectations to determine the success of the relationship.

TWO SYSTEMS

ASK **Ask the participants to explain the difference between the two covenants of law and grace as a way to review the previous session.**

Review Session 18 if necessary.

WHAT DO RELATIONSHIPS LOOK LIKE UNDER LAW?

EXPECTATIONS...

ASK **Describe a time when you did not meet another's expectation.**

Possible follow-up questions: How did they respond? How did you feel when they responded? What did you do?

PERFORMANCE...

ASK **How do you feel when you believe you have not met another's expectation?**

Possible answers: guilty, frustrated, regretful, worried, anxious, paranoid, resentful, useless, etc.

Possible follow-up question: What affect do these feelings have on your relationship? Possible answers: blaming, avoidance, loss of trust, emotional distance, dishonesty, denial, suspicion, bitterness, trying harder, giving up, etc.

SYSTEM OF FAILURE...

ASK **How do you feel when someone has not fulfilled your expectations?**

Identify negative emotions such as rejection, disrespect, anger, etc. Possible follow-up question: How do you treat them afterwards?

WHAT DO RELATIONSHIPS LOOK LIKE UNDER GRACE?

EXPECTATIONS...

ASK **What makes an expectation healthy versus unhealthy?**

Help the participants understand that there is nothing wrong with having expectations. If expectations become standards that govern how we treat others, then the relationship becomes toxic.

PERFORMANCE...

ASK **Describe a time when your behavior deserved judgment but someone treated you with grace. How did you feel? How did you respond to that person?**

Possible answers: I felt accepted, safe, loved, cared for, etc.

Possible responses: I relaxed and enjoyed the relationship, responded in kind, responded with gratitude, etc.

SYSTEM OF SUCCESS...

ASK **Describe your best relationship. What made it good? What would have made it better?**

KEY POINT: Law-based relationships demand perfect performance for acceptance.

KEY POINT: Relationships based on a law system will fail because the focus is on performance instead of identity.

KEY POINT: Graceful relationships do not depend on met expectations but are based on unconditional love and acceptance.

KEY POINT: Under grace, there is no pressure to perform for acceptance. Each of us can freely love others through the power of Jesus living in us.

KEY POINT: Grace-filled relationships are characterized by unconditional love, forgiveness, and freedom from guilt and condemnation.

ASK **How do you want to be treated in your relationships? What are the barriers (if any) that keep you from treating others that way?**

HOW DOES ACCOUNTABILITY FIT INTO RELATING UNCONDITIONALLY?

ASK **When you confess sin and/or struggles in your life to another person, how do you feel afterward?**

Possible answers: relief, clean, peace, healed, etc.

ASK **Describe a time when someone encouraged you and supported you when you confessed a sin or struggle. How did you feel?**

If they cannot remember an experience, share your own. This question allows the participants to make practical connections between the concept of grace and how grace is manifested through their thoughts, attitudes, and actions. Some examples: going from achieving to receiving, moving from demanding to gratitude, going from frustration to patience, etc.

....
KEY POINT:
Healthy accountability encourages other by reminding them of their true identity in Christ and placing the focus on Christ in them.

TRANSFORM

After meeting together, the Transform questions allow the participants to process the session's truths on their own. Review the participants' answers with them at the beginning of the next session.

PRAYER   (10 min.)

Since relationship and intimacy with God involves conversation, we encourage you to incorporate both individual and group prayer into your study.

EQUIPPING OTHERS
Multiplying Life

20

THEME

God multiplies His life in humanity by directing and empowering us to equip others.

SUMMARY

God desires the whole earth to be filled with His glory (His life). Through Jesus Christ, God has placed His life inside of us. A burning desire grows for others to experience Christ's life as we come to know and believe the truth about God, our design and purpose, and our relationship with God in Christ. God's glory spreads as we share Christ's life with others and equip them (make disciples). This process results in the multiplication and maturing of the body of Christ. Life Equippers enjoy an intimate walk with God, intentionally engage others in healthy relationships, and grow together in love and truth. Through the model Jesus displayed, we can share life with unbelievers and equip believers as they grow in their knowledge and understanding of Christ as their life.

TRANSFORM REVIEW — (10 min.)

1. What do the various ratings say about my expectations, disappointments, and rejection (directly or indirectly) of this person?

This question is designed to help the participants recognize how and to what extent they place others under law. If the participants have struggled with this exercise, give them an example from your personal life.

2. In what ways do I try to get my needs met through my most intimate relationships?

Possible answers: using sarcasm, exploding, whining, giving silent treatment, paying compliments, fishing for compliments, acting as a victim, etc.

3. What is standing in the way of surrendering my expectations of others to God?

Possible answers: pride, selfishness, fear, insecurity, false belief about what will satisfy, etc.

4. In what ways have I expressed grace in my relationships?

Possible answers: forgiving, over-looking an offense, encouraging, focusing on the other's identity over their behavior, serving, showing consideration, exhibiting empathy, etc.

TEACHING TIP:
Before beginning today's lesson, review the transform questions from Session 19: Relating Unconditionally. The participant should have answered these alone before coming together for this session.

CONNECT   (10 min.)

 TEACHING TIP:
Remember to listen, not teach.

ASK **What has God revealed to you since we last met?**

Discuss any additional revelations not covered in the Transform review.

ASK **Who has influenced you in a way that spurred growth in your Christian walk?**

This question encourages the participants to reflect on the people who have played an important role in their spiritual journey. Encourage them to recognize more than one person.

ASK **In what ways have they influenced you?**

Encourage the participants to describe the methods, behaviors, and/or activities that the other person(s) demonstrated.

 RENEW   (60 min.)

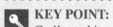 **KEY POINT:**
God's goal is to live in people and express His life through them, filling the earth with His glory.

GOD'S GOAL FOR HUMANITY

ASK **What does God's goal for humanity reveal about Him?**

God is love. He desires everyone to become containers and expressers of His love. If needed, refer to Session 1.

ASK **What role do we play in filling the earth with the glory of God?**

ASK **Do you have a desire to share Christ's life with others?**

This question is a quick yes or no but can give you an insight into the participants' view of their identity and desires. If the participants say no, use follow-up questions to explore the beliefs and emotions that are hindering them. Possible questions: What do you think is hindering you from that desire? What can change that desire?

ASK **How has your desire to share the good news with others changed since you have been in this study?**

ILLUSTRATION: MULTIPLICATION

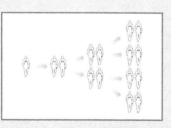

ASK **In regards to discipleship, how is multiplication more powerful than addition?**

Disciple makers who seek to enlarge their spheres of influence use addition as a means of growth. Whereas, disciple makers who equip others to do what they do use multiplication as a means of growth. Growth becomes exponential when disciples multiply. When addition is used, growth is much slower and limited by the original discipler's resources.

LIFE SHARED AND MULTIPLIED IN RELATIONSHIPS

ASK **Who influenced you to become a Christian? How did they influence you?**

ASK **Who has encouraged or discipled you in your growth as a Christian? Share about that experience.**

ASK **Who have you influenced to become a Christian?**

ASK **Who have you encouraged in their Christian walk?**

The last two questions may incite shame. Remind the participants to rest in their identity in Christ and explore these questions without condemnation.

ILLUSTRATION: SHARING AND EQUIPPING IN RELATIONSHIPS

Review the guide to this illustration on page 169 of the Living IN Jesus Participant's Guide. This illustration displays the different ways the life of Jesus can flow out of a Christian to unbelievers, young believers and mature believers.

OUR EXAMPLE FOR LIFE EQUIPPING – JESUS

ASK **Describe an interaction between Jesus and his disciples. How did He use truth? How did he display love and grace to them?**

Possible interactions: Jesus prayed for Peter (Luke 22:31-32). Jesus washed the disciple's feet (John 13:1-17). Jesus rebuked James and John for their desire to kill the Samaritans (Luke 9:53-55).

WALKING IN INTIMACY WITH THE FATHER

ASK **What does it mean to have an intimate walk with God?**

If needed, refer to Sessions 4, 11, or 13.

INTENTIONALLY ENGAGING OTHERS IN HEALTHY RELATIONSHIPS

ASK **Who has intentionally engaged you? What did he or she do that impacted you spiritually?**

KEY POINT:
God designed us to intentionally share Christ's life with others, leading unbelievers to salvation and encouraging believers to grow in their Christian walk.

KEY POINT:
Jesus' example of intimacy and intentionality guides us in how to multiply His life as He lives through us to equip others in the same way.

KEY POINT:
Through intimate fellowship with our Heavenly Father, we will know how He wants us to display and multiply His life and love in the world.

KEY POINT:
Life equipping is most effective within healthy, intentional relationships grounded in love and grace.

ASK How has the Holy Spirit prompted you to interact with another person? What did He want you to say or do?

ASK What person or persons has God placed on your heart to share the good news of Christ's indwelling life?

If the participants do not have an answer, encourage them to pray about a person and continue this journey in Transform question #3.

ASK How will you engage the person or persons you just named to join you in an equipping relationship?

Possible approaches: have conversations to discover their spiritual hunger and interest in growing; listen for cues to ask further questions about their desires; serve them where a need is indicated (home project, watch each other's kids, etc.); invite them to join you in growing together; etc.

GROWING TOGETHER IN LOVE AND TRUTH

ASK How has another person expressed love and truth to you?

ASK How does listening communicate love and enhance a relationship?

Possible answers: values people by showing interest in their lives; provides you with insight into how to encourage them; leads to a deeper connection when combined with follow-up questions, etc.

ASK What are benefits of asking questions as you equip others?

Possible benefits: engages the other person, causes them to think; honors them by acknowledging their input; invites further thinking and ownership of the truth; empowers the other person, etc.

KEY POINT:
Effective equipping relationships are always centered in love and truth as demonstrated by Jesus.

🦋 TRANSFORM   (10 min.)

After meeting together, the Transform questions allow the participants to process the session's truths on their own. For this last session, take a few moments to answer the questions with the participants before the final review.

1. What hindrances might keep me from equipping others?

The participants have the opportunity to identify barriers to building relationships. These barriers can be internal (shyness, fear of rejection, assuming false identities, lack of confidence, etc.) or external (limited connections with others, busy schedules, etc.). If needed, ask follow-up questions for the participants to fully explore the possible barriers. (e.g., "What fears do you have regarding making new relationships?", "What activities keep you from making new relationships?")

2. In which of my current relationships can I express God's life and love and share what He has done in my life?

The participants recognize the current opportunities to express Christ's life both in behavior and words. Possible follow-up question: In what ways can you express God's life to that person?

3. Take some time to listen to the Spirit. Is He placing a new person on my heart with whom I could build a healthy relationship? If so, who?

The participants are now led to pray about new opportunities to build healthy relationships and identify specific people through God's prompting.

4. In what ways could I go about building that relationship?

The participants now ask the Holy Spirit for specific, or practical ways to begin building a relationship. The participants may need coaching to describe the first step to building a relationship (make a call, start a longer conversation after church, invite for coffee or lunch, etc.). As the participants discover what they have in common with the prospective person, they can seek ways to deepen the relationship. In a new relationship, remember it is probably not a good idea to immediately ask the other person if you can disciple them using a book called *Living IN Jesus*. Wait on the Lord's timing.

TESTIMONIES AND NEXT STEPS

Take some time in this final session to celebrate what God has done on your journey of *Living IN Jesus*. Use these questions to promote sharing of testimonies and exploration of areas for further growth.

- What major truths did you learn?

- In what ways has God worked in your life during this course?

- How has this study helped deepen your intimacy with God?

- What concepts are still confusing to you?

- What truths do you struggle to believe?

- What truth is the Holy Spirit leading you to explore further from this study?

ABOUT THE AUTHORS

The Living IN Jesus study has been written by the combined effort of the counseling and coaching staff at Christian Families Today (CFT). CFT exists to educate and encourage men, women, and children in building biblically healthy lives and families. The truths found in this study are distilled from the Advanced Discipleship Training course and from nearly four decades of experience in counseling and coaching individuals to live out of Christ's life. CFT is a member of Network 220 (www.network220.org). Some diagrams and content in this publication have been adapted from Network 220 conference materials. Network 220 (named after Galatians 2:20) is an international network of churches, counseling ministries, and training ministries who are committed to the life-changing message of our new identity and life in Jesus Christ.

ADDITIONAL RESOURCES

TO FURTHER EQUIP THE LIFE EQUIPPER, THE FOLLOWING ARE AVAILABLE:

Grow in Grace Seminar: an expanded teaching of Romans 5-8 which sets forth a believer's identification with Christ in His death, burial, and resurrection. Through understanding how to appropriate one's identification in Christ, believers not only begin to understand the Exchanged Life, but also learn how to bring life's trials and tribulations to resolution. This seminar is presented quarterly at Christian Families Today's office in Newnan, GA.

Advanced Discipleship Training (ADT): provides a deeper and more comprehensive understanding of The Exchanged Life through teaching a believer's identification in Christ, learning how to build biblically healthy relationships based upon a believer's identification in Christ and learning how a believer can effectively share his or her identification in Christ with others. This training is conducted at Christian Families Today's office in Newnan, GA and internationally through the internet.

For more information on these opportunities and additional resources, visit our website at:

www.ChristianFamiliesToday.org